LIVING THE
SUPERCAR
DREAM

Published by Blink Publishing

3.25, The Plaza,

535 Kings Road,

Chelsea Harbour,

London, SW10 0SZ

www.blinkpublishing.co.uk

facebook.com/blinkpublishing

twitter.com/blinkpublishing

TPB – 978-1-910536-86-5

Ebook – 978-1-910536-89-6

A CIP catalogue of this book is available from the British Library.

Cover design by Emily Rough

Design by Steve Leard – leard.co.uk

Printed and bound in Italy

3 5 7 9 10 8 6 4 2

Papers used by Blink Publishing are natural, recyclable products made from wood grown in sustainable forests.
The manufacturing processes conform to the environmental regulations of the country of origin.

Every reasonable effort has been made to trace copyright holders of material reproduced in this book, but if
any have been inadvertently overlooked the publishers would be glad to hear from them.

Blink Publishing is an imprint of the Bonnier Publishing Group
www.bonnierpublishing.co.uk

LIVING THE SUPERCAR DREAM

76 CARS, 14 COUNTRIES AND 1 DREAM

FROM POPULAR YOUTUBE CHANNEL

BLINK
bringing you closer

WELCOME TO MY WORLD — 08

ROAD TRIP 01
LONDON CALLING — 10
Aston Martin DBS — 14
McLaren F1 — 16
Rolls-Royce Phantom — 18
BMW i8 — 20
McLaren 650S Spider — 22
Jaguar XJ220 — 24

ROAD TRIP 02
DESTINATION EUROPE — 26
Ferrari FF — 30
Bentley Bentayga — 32
Mercedes-Maybach S600 — 34
Aston Martin Rapide S — 36
Audi RS 6 — 38

ROAD TRIP 03
GERMANY –
SPEED AND PERFORMANCE — 40
Audi S8 Plus — 44
Koenigsegg One:1 — 46
Porsche 918 Spyder — 48
Audi R8 V10 Plus — 50
Bugatti Veyron 16.4 Grand
Sport Vitesse — 52

ROAD TRIP 04
ALPINE ADVENTURE — 54
Porsche Cayman GT4 — 58
McLaren 570S — 60
Ferrari 488 GTB — 62
Mercedes-AMG GT S — 64
Lamborghini Huracán LP610-4 — 66

ROAD TRIP 05
DESIGNS ON ITALY — 68
Ferrari LaFerrari — 72
Pagani Zonda S — 74
Lamborghini Miura SV — 76
SCG 003 S — 78
Alfa Romeo 8C Competizione — 80
Ferrari F40 — 82

ROAD TRIP 06
MONACO, BABY! — 84
Rolls-Royce Dawn — 88
Ferrari 250 GTO — 90
Renault Twizy — 92
Ferrari 458 Speciale — 94
Mercedes-Benz 300 SL Gullwing — 96

ROAD TRIP 07
DUBAI DREAM — 98
Koenigsegg Regera — 102
Lamborghini Veneno — 104
Mercedes-Benz G 63 AMG — 106
Pagani Huayra — 108
Mercedes-Benz SLR McLaren
Stirling Moss — 110
Maserati MC12 — 112

ROAD TRIP 08
DESERT OUTRUN — 114
Mercedes-Benz G 63 AMG 6x6 — 118
W Motors Lykan HyperSport — 120
Lamborghini Aventador LP700-4 — 122
Aston Martin One-77 — 124
Porsche Carrera GT — 126

ROAD TRIP 09
INTO THE EAST 128
Lexus LFA 132
Nissan GT-R Nismo 134
Honda NSX 136
Lamborghini Murciélago 138
Nissan Skyline R34 GT-R 140

ROAD TRIP 10
WEST COAST AMERICA 142
Tesla Model S P90D 146
Ford GT 148
SSC Ultimate Aero 150
Mustang Eleanor 152
Hennessey Venom GT 154

ROAD TRIP 11
EAST COAST AMERICA 156
Range Rover Autobiography 160
Ferrari Testarossa 162
Rolls-Royce Wraith 164
Bentley Continental GT V8 S 166
Cadillac CTS-V 168

ROAD TRIP 12
MAKING TRACKS IN PORTUGAL 170
McLaren P1 174
Porsche 911 GT3 RS 176
Chevrolet Corvette Z06 178
McLaren 675LT 180
Ferrari F12tdf 182
BAC Mono 184

ROAD TRIP 13
FRANCE AND FURIOUS 186
Pagani Zonda R 190
Ferrari FXX K 192
Aston Martin Vulcan 194
McLaren P1 GTR 196
Lamborghini Sesto Elemento 198

ROAD TRIP 14
BEST OF BRITISH 200
Lotus Evora 400 204
Caterham 620S 206
Morgan Aero 8 208
Zenos E10 S 210
Ariel Atom 500 212
Morgan 3 Wheeler 214

DREAM GARAGE 216

SHMEE150'S SUPERCAR BOOK APP

• • •

LIVE THE SUPERCAR DREAM BEYOND THE PRINTED PAGE! Experience a thrilling road trip around the world of supercars with the Shmee150 Supercar Book App! Tim Burton, aka Shmee150, provides an insight into some of the fastest and most luxurious cars ever made through exclusive video footage and picture galleries.

All you have to do is download the free app from the iTunes App Store or Google Play Store, launch the app and point your device's camera at the pages with this special icon on them. Then watch the content come to life on your screen!

Scan this page now for your first special feature!

The Shmee150 Supercar Book App requires an Internet connection to be downloaded and can be used on iPhone, iPad or Android devices. For direct links to download the app and further information, visit www.blinkpublishing.co.uk.

WELCOME TO MY WORLD

When I was a kid sitting in the back seat of the car on family journeys, my dad would always be quick to point out interesting or exciting cars. For my young eyes, it was like catching a rare bird in flight. If I was slow off the mark, I would miss that glorious moment completely and so I quickly learned to keep a close eye on the road. Over time, I learned what these incredible sleek and often thunderous vehicles were called. It became my role to reel off the names, along with the power statistics and I took great pride in getting the details just right. From there, a love affair was born that has come to define everything I do.

In short, I am passionate about supercars and this book is my celebration of that world.

But spotting a Bugatti in the wild is one thing. Getting behind the wheel of one is quite another and first I had to create the opportunity. After completing my A-levels at 18, I grew an online electronics retail venture that developed into a London high street shop. The business quickly changed hands and, following a stint as a ski instructor in New Zealand, I found a position with an investment consultancy firm in the City of London. It might've been far from supercars but the experience inspired an ambition to work in a field that meant so much to me.

Whenever I saw an interesting car around town I would take a picture of it and post it to spotters' forums online. As for the name Shmee150, it was something I had always used and it felt like a natural name for the YouTube channel I went on to establish in 2010. I shot my first video at a Top Gear magazine event in London as a test for my new camera… and that's when I knew that I had found my calling.

Today, my Shmee150 channel is bigger than I could have ever imagined. It's clear that millions of you share my passion and I'm delighted to provide a focal point, no matter where you are in the world. YouTube is where I share exclusive automotive content that's tailor-made for you. Whether I'm attending an invitation-only preview or a trade launch, test-driving a new vehicle, taking to the road on a big adventure or pushing the rev needle into the red on a track day, I've got the world of supercars covered. What's more, I'm lucky enough to have begun my own personal collection of cars.

With careful buying and selling, heading upwards all the way, the Shmeemobiles that have graced my garage range from my original Renault Clio 1.2 and a BMW 1 Series to more recent acquisitions such as the Ferrari FF and McLaren 675LT Spider. At the same time, I've expanded my social media networks to connect and converse about whatever's hot on four wheels. Now, as this unbelievable journey continues to gather momentum, it gives me great pleasure to introduce the book in your hands – my guide to living the supercar dream.

PERFORMANCE STATISTICS UNLOCKED

This book is intended to get you up close and personal with my favourite supercars. Alongside my first-hand accounts of how it really feels to be shifting through the gears in a high performance vehicle, you'll find technical details to provide a full picture of each car's capability. Here's a quick guide to what you can expect.

TORQUE

The turning force when power is delivered to the axle. So a car with a lot of torque can seriously shift from a standstill, and keep on building speed. Here, torque is measured in Newton metres (Nm).

ENGINE SIZE

I'll focus on two aspects of an engine's characteristics here. The first is a litre (l) measurement, which reflects the total volume of air the pistons can sweep through the cylinders in one cycle as part of the fuel combustion process. Depending on the vehicle, an engine can feature anything from two to 12 cylinders. These can be laid out in one row, known as a 'straight' engine, a 'V' formation or a 'flat' configuration (with horizontally-opposed pistons). The number associated with each type of engine represents how many cylinders it contains.

BHP

This stands for brake horse power. When it comes to cars, it's a measurement of how hard the engine works.

In the pages that follow, I've pulled together the most exotic locations and the very best vehicles from my travels around the globe to create a dream road trip. Each destination highlights different demands from car and driver. From the streets of London to the West Coast of America, these are theatrical stages to showcase the finest high-end automobiles in the world. I'll introduce you to the essential places to see and be seen in alongside circuits to master in a bid to nail the best lap times.

Along with a selection of my standout first-hand experiences – and a description of all-out power, performance and handling, as well as style and comfort – I intend to share the very best qualities in the supercars I've handpicked for each occasion. This round-the-world journey knows no bounds and it's a pleasure to have you along for the ride.

Above all, I want you to get the inside view of how it really feels to be in the driving seat. I might be living the supercar dream but without doubt it's one to be shared – and that just makes the experience even more magical. So, without further ado, let's jump in, buckle up, and prepare to start your engine…

LON

ROAD TRIP 01

DON
CALLING

LONDON CALLING

• • •

The UK's capital is one of the world's greatest tourist attractions. From Buckingham Palace to the Tower of London, the Houses of Parliament, Hyde Park and the river Thames, London is rich in history and culture. At the same time, it's become a popular destination for anyone looking to spot seriously cool supercars.

At any time of year, you'll catch sight of high-performance vehicles on the road or parked outside exclusive clubs and restaurants – if you know where to look. Come the summer time, however, the city undergoes a transformation. Then, supercar owners from across the world take their finest vehicles to the capital to create an informal street celebration of automotive exclusivity and state-of-the-art design.

Knightsbridge is perhaps the most popular hotspot, particularly from June through to August. Anywhere from the side streets behind the world-famous Harrods department store and outside The Park Tower hotel to The Dorchester Hotel or Lowndes Square, you can expect to spot anything from a Lamborghini Aventador LP700-4 to a Pagani Huayra. And if you're not sure where to look, just follow the noise! For these are supercars that like to make their presence known. Throughout the summer months, across Knightsbridge, Mayfair, Park Lane, Chelsea, Westminster and South Kensington, you can guarantee that an engine roar will quickly draw a crowd.

In kicking off my series of around-the-world road trips in London, I'm looking to select a host of supercars that you can expect to see in public spaces. These are cars that embody London's international spirit, diversity and taste. It's also a chance to celebrate the best of British manufacturers, who often lead the way in terms of automotive luxury, sophistication, design splendour and, of course, incredible performance power.

SHMEE150'S SELECTION

...

ASTON MARTIN DBS

McLAREN F1

ROLLS-ROYCE PHANTOM

BMW i8

McLAREN 650S SPIDER

JAGUAR XJ220

ASTON MARTIN

DBS

AMR 1A

ENGINE TYPE	5,935cc V12
NUMBER OF CYLINDERS	12
FUEL TYPE	Premium Unleaded
MAXIMUM OUTPUT	380 kW (517 PS/510 bhp) at 6,500 rpm
MAXIMUM TORQUE	570 Nm (420 lb-ft) at 5,750 rpm
SPRINT TIME TO 62MPH	4.3 seconds
TOP SPEED	190 mph
GEARBOX TYPE	Six-speed manual transmission or six-speed automatic transmission

Let's kick off with a classic. In my view, the Aston Martin DBS is one of the best-sounding luxury supercars in the business. Even with the engine idling you could be listening to a hive of angry bees. Then you hit the throttle and the snarl could wake the dead. It's formidable, sonorous and thrilling; guaranteed to make the hairs on the back of your neck stand on end, whether you're behind the wheel or simply witnessing this magnificent car as it rushes across Sloane Street.

It's fair to say that Aston Martin has form when it comes to setting the benchmark. James Bond didn't jump into one without good reason. He's a Brit with impeccable taste and an appreciation of what a 6.0-litre V12 engine can produce in anger. With a six-speed transmission and chest-compressing torque as you accelerate, the ride from 0–62 mph will take just 4.3 seconds. Make no mistake, this is a seriously powerful performance car. It also happens to look like a timeless work of art.

Aston Martin has a rich history to call upon and this is evident in the design of the modern-day DBS. It drew heavily on the iconic DB9, which makes it unbelievably cool in my book, but with a more aggressive edge in its sleek, prowling design. From a bystander's point of view this is the car you can't help but stop and admire but it's only when you slip into the driving seat that its true majesty becomes apparent.

The Aston Martin DBS is styled in a way that makes you feel like a million dollars. The interior is stunning, beautifully illuminated after dark and primed for both comfort and driving confidence. Pull away in this Bond-mobile and I guarantee you'll feel as if you're on a mission on Her Majesty's Secret Service.

The DBS also provides one crucial element missed on some other ultra-high-performance cars by handling like an extension of your own body. It's all very well having masses of power at your bidding, but the car needs to enable the driver to harness it. Here, the Aston Martin DBS comes into its own, with a series of driving modes that cater for a wide range of skills and conditions. With pitch-perfect balance, weight distribution and grip, this synthesis of raw power and design excellence guarantees maximum driving pleasure whether you're at speed on the open road or cruising through the UK's capital.

ENGINE TYPE	6,064cc V12
NUMBER OF CYLINDERS	12
FUEL TYPE	Premium Unleaded
MAXIMUM OUTPUT	468 kW (636 PS/627 bhp) at 7,400 rpm
MAXIMUM TORQUE	651 Nm (480 lb-ft) at 5,600 rpm
SPRINT TIME TO 62MPH	3.2 seconds
TOP SPEED	243 mph
GEARBOX TYPE	Six-speed manual transmission

H ere is a world-record holder that needs no introduction. It sports the name of one of my favourite manufacturers, a company celebrated for melding innovation, engineering, design and detail – on both road and track. As a Formula 1 team, for example, McLaren produced the peerless MP4/4, a championship car so closely associated with legendary drivers Ayrton Senna and Alain Prost that when the manufacturer announced a move into production cars it's fair to say that excitement levels reached fever pitch. And so the McLaren F1 first went into production in 1994. This was the result of a commitment to build the finest sports car the world has ever seen and the company delivered.

From the moment you set eyes on the McLaren F1, notably the central driving position within the three-seater, carbon-fibre monocoque, it's clear that this is a high-performance vehicle that demands attention. The sleek, curved and organically aerodynamic design is breathtaking and makes no compromise. Even the scissor action of the doors as they open upwards feels in keeping with the car's muscular assembly. Then you consider the McLaren racing heritage and learn that in 1998 the V12-powered F1 set the record for the world's fastest production car by reaching a speed of 231 mph – and that was with the rev limiter enabled!

There are few supercars in the world that are as instantly recognisable as a McLaren and even fewer

McLAREN F1

that command such instant, all-round respect. On the streets of London, the sight or sound of an F1 quickly commands the eyes and ears of passers-by and for this reason alone it makes the cut for my road tour of the capital.

The central driving position might take some getting used to at first, but it's there for a reason. Once you're behind the wheel the utility of the driving position becomes evident in the visibility it affords, as well as the ability to position the car with absolute precision. In fact, when you're threading through some of the capital's narrow streets, you'll start to wonder why every car doesn't follow this ground-breaking design. Whether you're alone or flanked by passengers

– positioned just behind your line of sight – it feels like a natural position to maintain optimum control.

At speed, the F1 is both a revelation and a constant reminder that focus is required at all times. It's an intensely powerful beast with the potential to outstrip your driving capabilities should you dare to get ahead of yourself. Personally, I revel in the challenge of approaching what is sometimes referred to as the first ever hypercar. It takes respect – for yourself, the vehicle and your surroundings – as well as patience and courage. Get it right and an automotive wonder like the McLaren F1 will reward you with a high-performance driving experience that you'll never forget.

ROLLS-ROYCE
PHANTOM

This is the very last word in luxury on wheels. The Rolls-Royce Phantom has been in existence for almost a century now. Every new edition meets exacting standards in prestige and power. It's unlike any other luxury car and a cut above the rest in many different ways.

The Rolls-Royce Phantom Drophead and the Rolls-Royce Phantom Drophead Coupé were based on the revered 2003 Phantom luxury saloon. The Drophead is more compact and arguably appeals to those who prefer to give the chauffeur a day off so they can do

their own driving, while the Coupé offers a convertible experience. Despite the differences, both editions call upon the basic Phantom chassis, V12 engine and bodywork design.

Each car is finished according to the customer's specifications. In keeping with any work of art or fine jewellery, the unique combination of colour, paint (applied by hand, of course), wood and interior leatherwork means that no two Phantoms are alike. In an exclusive neighbourhood like Knightsbridge, this kind of pedigree is never overlooked, which is why I have featured

ENGINE TYPE	6,749cc V12
NUMBER OF CYLINDERS	12
FUEL TYPE	Premium Unleaded
MAXIMUM OUTPUT	338 kW (460 PS/453 bhp) at 5,350 rpm
MAXIMUM TORQUE	720 Nm (531 lb-ft) at 3,500 rpm
SPRINT TIME TO 62MPH	5.9 seconds
TOP SPEED	150 mph (governed)
GEARBOX TYPE	Eight-speed automatic transmission

BMW i8

The high-performance or luxury car leads the way in automotive engineering and design. It's here that innovation and breakthroughs occur, slowly trickling down to mass-produced cars. When a car appears that does something differently and to great effect, it offers us all a glimpse of the future. Which brings me to the BMW i8. It's a hybrid sports car but, before we get to the power delivery, one of the coolest things about it is how they've managed to retain the 'concept' look. In terms of appearance, it looks like a BMW that's accessed a time machine and popped back to show everyone what's in store a few years from now. It isn't preposterously futuristic, but rather the silken lines, poise and confidence in the design are simply extensions of where we are with cars today.

As for the performance innovation, the i8 features just a 1.5-litre turbocharged engine. This is a rear-wheel-drive power unit, but it's not the only form of propulsion – and this is where the engineering wizardry takes centre stage. The front end is where the future lies. This is where you'll find an electric motor – and it packs a considerable punch. Combined with a lithium-ion battery pack, the BMW i8 can produce an astonishing 357 bhp. It's lightweight, punchy, frighteningly quick and, above all, a sure sign that high-performance vehicles are successfully evolving to embrace serious energy efficiency. That the i8, a car capable of 0–62 mph in 4.4 seconds and a top speed of 155 mph, can also turn in 135 miles per gallon is frankly incredible and hugely encouraging.

On jumping behind the wheel, having drawn down the dihedral door, you'll find yourself in reassuringly BMW territory. Design functionality is very important here and you'll find the interior is kitted out to be both practical and pleasing on the eye. There are rear seats, should you wish to take passengers for a cruise around the London streets, as well as boot space behind the petrol engine. As soon as you pull away on battery power, however, marvelling at the silent delivery, your attention will be firmly on what this incredible hybrid car is capable of producing on the road.

The good news is that this isn't a sports car that pays for its low-carbon emissions with a reduced entertainment value. The i8 handles like any petrol-fuelled contemporary, providing traction, grip and epic handling abilities. That such a fuel-efficient vehicle can deliver a high-performance driving experience is testament to BMW. It's also a sign that cars at the cutting edge of engineering and design will still have a place in urban spaces. This is why the i8 is such a vital addition to our line-up of London's signature performance or luxury vehicles.

ENGINE TYPE	1,499cc turbocharged Inline-3 engine + hybrid synchronous motor
NUMBER OF CYLINDERS	3
FUEL TYPE	Premium Unleaded / Electric Charge
MAXIMUM OUTPUT	266 kW (362 PS/357 bhp)
MAXIMUM TORQUE	570 Nm (420 lb-ft)
SPRINT TIME TO 62MPH	4.4 seconds
TOP SPEED	155 mph (governed) (hybrid)
GEARBOX TYPE	Six-speed automatic transmission

London is my home town and so, for this venture, I have to feature what was once one of my prized Shmeemobiles. The McLaren 650S Spider joined my stable of thoroughbred supercars towards the end of 2014. It replaced my McLaren 12C, which surprised many. I'm always keen to point out that I absolutely loved the 12C. I found it faultless in every way. In fact, the only reason I decided to upgrade is because McLaren have surpassed themselves in producing a car that took everything from the 12C that worked so well and made it better on so many vital points. In the same way, I went on to switch the 650S Spider for the 675LT for the simple reason that it offered a track-focused version of the McLaren Super Series. In short, I'm a huge fan of the marque, and proud to have called them all Shmeemobiles over recent years.

With the 650S Spider, you have an extra 25 bhp, more torque, improved suspension and bodywork refinements that fit in with McLaren's stunning P1 hypercar. Above all, as it's a Spider, I had the opportunity to ride with no roof over my head. It was an irresistible prospect and I never looked back. I'm also able to speak from experience when I say that driving the 650S Spider through London was a guaranteed event. Not just for the driver but anyone with an appreciation of automotive engineering and design. In west London, it's rare to travel more than a block at the wheel of a supercar without someone whipping out a camera phone. And it wasn't just those who share a passion for high-performance cars who were interested. I can assure you that the roar of a McLaren in a narrow street flanked by high buildings is something nobody can ignore. The din is incredible and ricochets off the walls like the sound of an avalanche in a canyon. My 650S Spider was also mantis green – you could see it from a mile off.

Inside the car, McLaren's attention to detail ensures that everything was present and correct. The display behind the wheel offers a pleasingly large radial rev counter while the console screen in the centre of the dash provides a menu of controls primed for usability on the move. The seats are comfortable and robust and from the moment you buckle up it feels like this car is about to take you for a ride you'll never forget.

The 650S Spider boasts a 3.8-litre V8 engine capable of producing a breathtaking 641 bhp. The torque is intense and can propel the car from a standing start to 62 mph in a blistering 3.2 seconds. It's a very different car to the other McLaren I've selected here, although the racing DNA is present and you feel it from the moment you squeeze the accelerator. The 650S Spider is capable of shining on both track and road, while simply cruising through the capital's streets will prove to be an equally satisfying experience. With the top down, on a summer's evening, you'll feel like the city is yours for the taking.

ENGINE TYPE	3,799cc Twin-Turbo V8
NUMBER OF CYLINDERS	8
FUEL TYPE	Premium Unleaded
MAXIMUM OUTPUT	478 kW (650 PS/641 bhp) at 7,250 rpm
MAXIMUM TORQUE	678 Nm (500 lb-ft) at 6,000 rpm
SPRINT TIME TO 62MPH	3.2 seconds
TOP SPEED	204 mph
GEARBOX TYPE	Seven-speed automatic transmission

McLAREN

650S SPIDER

JAGUAR
XJ220

his is one of the poster cars for a generation. Quite literally – when it roared into life back in 1992, a poster of this legendary motor graced many bedroom walls. Back in the day, the Jaguar XJ220 was considered state-of-the-art for many good reasons. It certainly fuelled my devotion to high-performance vehicles and the chance to drive one through the streets of London was a long-held ambition come true. Even before I introduce you to the car, I can say with confidence that it's a sure-fire entry for my road trip around the UK's capital.

The XJ220 was very much a product of its age. The long, chiselled design created a supercar blueprint for many years to come. Naturally, automotive construction has evolved, introducing more organic lines and defined postures and yet this spectacular Jaguar still commands respect among anyone who appreciates the combination of speed, power and aerodynamic design.

Jumping in really does feel like heading back to the future. The dashboard might look dated now with its big switches and dials, but at the time it was mind-blowingly advanced. As for the drive, it's fair to say you can expect a handful. The gearshifts aren't easy, the clutch is a lot of work and you sense the potential power could overwhelm you with one wrong move. At the same time, the car allows you to get a feel of things. Yes, the XJ220 is big and some might say heavy, but that stops being an issue as you begin to pick up confidence and speed. Then something extraordinary happens to the way in which the car performs. Turning in becomes intuitive, as does the handling out of a corner and you learn just where to find the sweet spot on the throttle. That's when everything comes together and this classic old Jag starts to sing.

With a top speed of 217 mph, the XJ220 is quite capable of outrunning many modern-day supercars. At the same time, its sheer size and unmistakable shape commands fond memories as much as awe and respect when you take it on a glory run through the streets of London.

ENGINE TYPE	3,498cc Twin-Turbo V6
NUMBER OF CYLINDERS	6
FUEL TYPE	Premium Unleaded
MAXIMUM OUTPUT	404 kW (550 PS/542 bhp) at 7,200 rpm
MAXIMUM TORQUE	641 Nm (473 lb-ft) at 4,500 rpm
SPRINT TIME TO 62MPH	3.6 seconds
TOP SPEED	217 mph
GEARBOX TYPE	Five-speed manual transmission

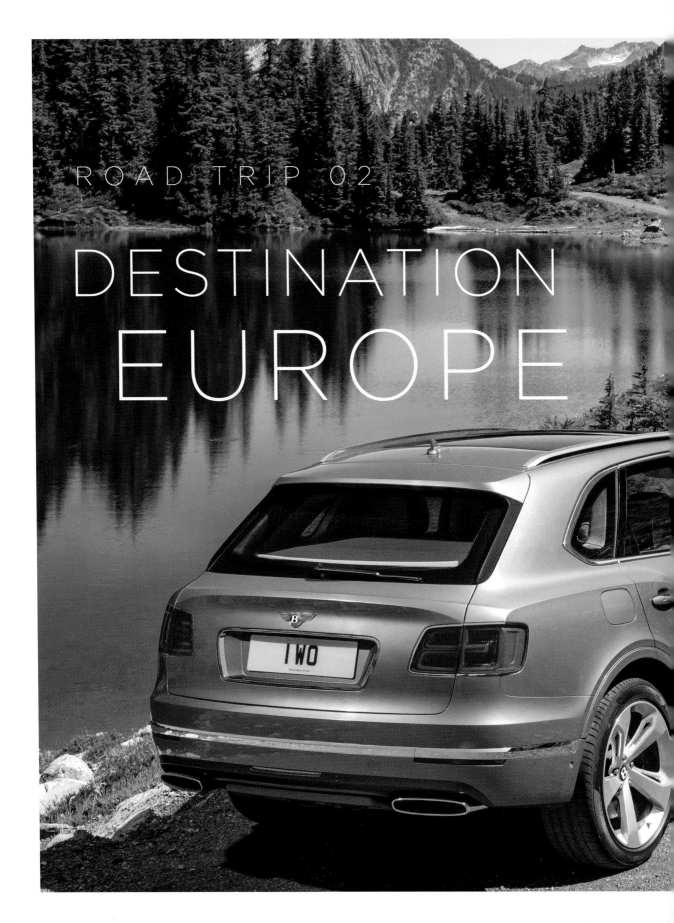

ROAD TRIP 02

DESTINATION
EUROPE

DESTINATION EUROPE

• • •

A ll road trips set my pulse racing with anticipation. The prospect of firing up one of my supercars for an adventure often means I'm good to go at the crack of dawn. I always want to make sure everything is ready before setting off, especially with a long journey ahead.

With my base in London and a calendar crammed with international trips, I'm used to heading out of the capital *en route* to a Channel port. Before I can say 'breakfast' I've loaded my car onto the Eurotunnel le Shuttle and we're off! Once I've reached the Continent, it's vital that I'm not distracted from

driving on the right by worrying about whether I'm on the correct route. Preparation is key and even in vehicles with top-flight navigation systems I find it's worth taking a little time in advance to know exactly where I'm heading. At the very least, in cars this good, it frees you up to enjoy the ride.

So, for this trip I'm spotlighting luxury transports that are equally capable of catering for a long stretch away as they are for their blistering performance capabilities. I'm looking for comfort as much as space here, but ultimately nothing must compromise that sense of power.

FERRARI FF

BENTLEY BENTAYGA

MERCEDES-MAYBACH S600

ASTON MARTIN RAPIDE S

AUDI RS 6

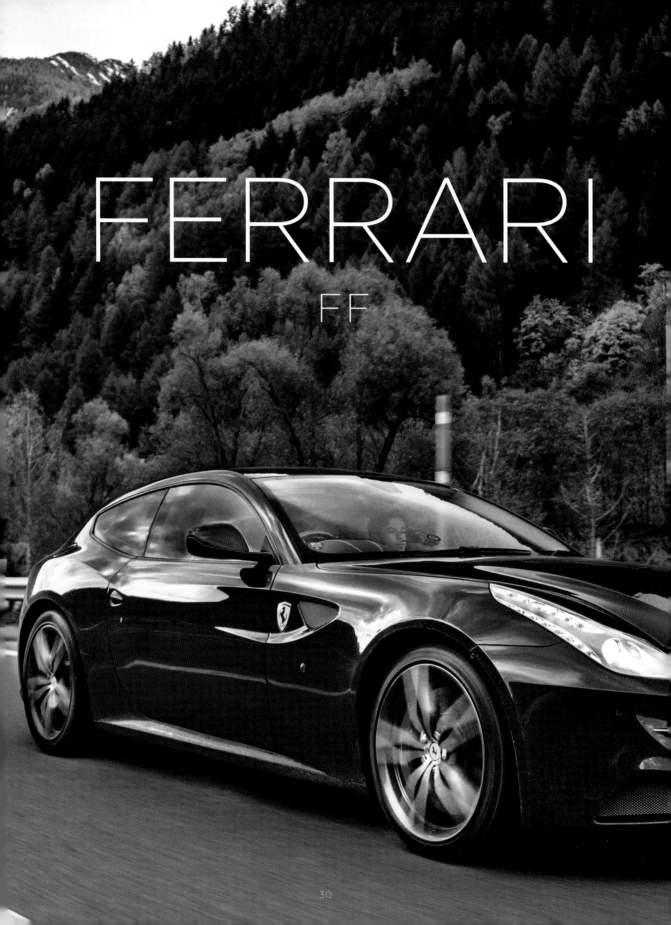

FERRARI

FF

y first choice out of the garage is from my own fleet of Shmeemobiles. The Ferrari FF sits alongside my McLaren 675LT as a personal favourite, but for very different reasons. While the McLaren is very much for special occasions, I consider the Ferrari to be for everyday use. In particular, I recognised its potential as the perfect supercar for road trips that involved hours behind the wheel.

The FF features a 652 bhp 6.3-litre V12 engine, so the performance and exhaust notes are immense. I also love the look of this grand tourer although I'm well aware that not everybody shares my passion. With a hatchback rear, it's been described as a two-door estate car and while that's certainly a reflection of the car's luggage capacity, I think it's a strikingly handsome beast. In my opinion, the FF is by far the coolest way for four people to travel in style.

With a bespoke Le Mans Blue paint finish and crema interior, both of which set off the familiar Scuderia shields in style, I will admit this outstanding colour combination first sold the car to me. But then I got to see it up close and personal and that's when I knew I had found my vehicle of choice for long-haul stretches. It's an elegant-looking car without a doubt and in some ways calls upon a design you'd normally associate with a coupe. If you consider the sheer size, coupled with that monstrous engine, you'll see that Ferrari has created a vehicle that's as spacious as it is ferocious. With the rear seats folded you can comfortably accommodate anything from skis to the family dog and still be assured of premium pace and handling.

On the road the FF is a mighty machine indeed. It's capable of screaming from 0–62 mph in 3.7 seconds and can hit speeds of 208 mph. That's a heck of a lot of punch and grunt by any supercar standard and leaves the critics open-mouthed in awe. It might be a like-it or loathe-it kind of car, but I love it. So long as you feel good behind the wheel and it serves the purpose you set out to achieve, nothing else really matters. Where some might look at long stretches on the road and feel a sense of dread, in the FF it's a joy. On that basis alone, I heartily recommend it.

ENGINE TYPE	6.262cc V12
NUMBER OF CYLINDERS	12
FUEL TYPE	Premium Unleaded
MAXIMUM OUTPUT	486 kW (660 PS/652 bhp) at 8,000 rpm
MAXIMUM TORQUE	683 Nm (504 lb-ft) at 6,000 rpm
SPRINT TIME TO 62MPH	3.7 seconds
TOP SPEED	208 mph
GEARBOX TYPE	Seven-speed automatic transmission

BENTLEY
BENTAYGA

This was Bentley's entry into the SUV market. Given the marque's pedigree and pledge to meet the luxury end, it was an exciting prospect. One look at the Bentayga, notably the handsome bonnet and upright grille, leaves you in no doubt of the DNA of this vehicle. Everything else about it might look like a 4x4, but the front end is effectively royalty. The design and styling cues might polarise opinion, much like the Ferrari FF, but it's quite clearly a Bentley and that brings certain delicious expectations.

Starting with the performance capability: the Bentayga boasts a 600-bhp, 12-cylinder Twin-Turbo W12, which, straight away, tells you that this is no ordinary SUV. It's incredibly powerful, capable of 0–62 mph in under 5 seconds and a top speed of 187 mph. That's more than enough to scare the sheep on a jaunt through the countryside, but in my opinion this is one SUV better-suited to long-haul road trips than cross-field mudfests.

For while the Bentayga packs an impressive degree of

ENGINE TYPE	5,950cc Twin-Turbo W12
NUMBER OF CYLINDERS	12
FUEL TYPE	Premium Unleaded
MAXIMUM OUTPUT	447 kW (608 PS/600 bhp) at 5,000–6,000 rpm
MAXIMUM TORQUE	900 Nm (664 lb-ft) at 1,350 rpm
SPRINT TIME TO 62MPH	4.1 seconds
TOP SPEED	187 mph
GEARBOX TYPE	Eight-speed automatic transmission

punch and grip, it is also a Bentley. As soon as you climb inside and take in the chrome, leather and handcrafted wood surfaces, it becomes completely apparent that high-end comfort is the key to the appeal. The seats alone boast 22 different adjustable settings and, while the console offers an array of control options, it's the careful application of technology that makes it all look so simple. Passengers in the rear, for example, will be delighted to find tailor-made Wi-Fi tablets mounted on the headrests. These are completely detachable, can be used outside the vehicle and are sure to be one of the car's most popular features. The optional dash clock is another standout detail. This bespoke mechanical timepiece might come at a price, but watching it rotate to wind itself up is a joy.

This is seriously refined, luxury driving, with an option to sit five, so plenty of room for the nanny, bodyguard or butler. Yes, it's posh and though storage isn't a feature you would normally consider with a vehicle of this calibre, it's been designed to carry a lot of stuff. The boot, in particular, is deep enough to hold enough picnic hampers to cater for a large party. In fact, Bentley offer a three-compartment hamper as an additional feature, one of which can keep your Champagne bottle chilled along with bespoke flutes that feature Bentley's logo on the base. If this sounds like the kind of circle you mix in, or if you just want a lot of luggage room, the Bentayga really is pleasingly practical.

The trimmings are enough to distract you from the fact that it's in the supercar league – until you hit the road. Then this supreme SUV comes into its own in terms of the kind of torque and power that will see you through those long journeys with confidence as well as style. The precision built into the power steering combined with a responsive eight-speed transmission delivers a truly seamless and impeccable drive. And, as you might expect from a Bentley, it's as smooth as butter.

Ultimately, the Bentayga can be summed up in four words: craftsmanship, prestige, usability and power. It's a one-of-a-kind combination that comes with a sizeable price tag, but for those who can afford to slip behind the wheel, I guarantee it'll furnish a supreme experience that's worth every penny.

ENGINE TYPE	5,980cc Twin-Turbo V12
NUMBER OF CYLINDERS	12
FUEL TYPE	Premium Unleaded
MAXIMUM OUTPUT	390 kW (530 PS/523 bhp) at 4,900–5,300 rpm
MAXIMUM TORQUE	830 Nm (612 lb-ft) at 1,900–4,000 rpm
SPRINT TIME TO 62MPH	5.0 seconds
TOP SPEED	155 mph (governed)
GEARBOX TYPE	Seven-speed automatic transmission

t's claimed that this is the world's most luxurious, high-powered saloon car. That's quite a boast but a first inspection of the model I've selected for my long haul into Europe does impress enormously. The Mercedes-Maybach S600 exists to compete with the likes of Rolls-Royce, which gives you some insight into the kind of vehicle under the spotlight here. It's certainly stately but the 6.0-litre, Twin-Turbo V12 engine, 523 bhp and 830 Nm of torque ensures it also packs one hell of a punch. I'm really excited about featuring this car as one of my choices for this road trip. Not only does it provide unsurpassable comfort for the driver and passengers – essential if you're driving for long durations – there's also some serious power under the bonnet.

The exterior is all about the promise of what this car contains. It's as solid as it is sleek with an air of refinement and gravitas in its design and aerodynamic styling. Even before you open the driver door, as reassuringly heavy as

a piano lid but yielding with graceful ease, you just know that you're about to behold the last word in automotive luxury. Behind the wood-finished steering wheel, two large radial displays and a central digital menu greet you. It looks timeless, combining tradition and technology, which is entirely in keeping with the vibe the Germans have set out to achieve.

As for the controls, there's a great deal to take in and yet everything is laid out intuitively. Take the seat adjusters. Often these can be confusing and in many cars it can be a question of trial and error before you find the right position. Here, the door-mounted switches are gathered within a subtle chrome plate shaped like the seat itself. So, if I want to bolster the lumbar support, for example, I know exactly what to press. It's a nice visual touch, deceptively simple, but it ramps up this car's usability factor no end. Another discreet panel, tucked just behind the steering wheel, provides a bank of assist controls for everything from parking to steering, including a 360-degree camera, car-proximity awareness

MERCEDES-MAYBACH
S600

and night vision. Many of these work in conjunction with the dashboard monitor, and I have to admit that I cannot stop playing with the camera, which proves surprisingly useful in tight streets and parking garages.

As customers for this car may well choose to have a chauffeur, absolutely everything is geared towards the driver. If you're travelling in the rear seats, for example, and don't wish to lift a finger to adjust the headrest, Jeeves can do it all for you at the touch of a button. At the same time, you have every option to determine your own comfort settings, which are duplicated in the back, of course. This includes a switch to shift the front passenger seat forward if you need more legroom and the ability to recline your seat flat. It really is a delight to explore and enjoy. In particular, I love the cooling and heating system incorporated into the cup holders and the foldable tables. There's even a mini-fridge. Naturally, everything tucks away to maintain the sense of luxury and refinement you would expect from a car of this calibre.

In short, there is absolutely no way you can become restless or uncomfortable in the S600. It's even fitted with an active body control. This means you can determine whether you'd like to feel the car perform in anger or cocoon yourself in luxury as if gliding on air.

While some might thrive on the sense of power, balance and speed, others will prefer to tune out from their surroundings completely. The car allows for just that and everything in between, together with its active exhaust valve control that determines whether you prefer your driving experience to be audibly rowdy or regal. Everything is adjustable to provide maximum comfort.

For the purposes of reaching the European mainland, this is one of a very select number of transports for me. Luxury and comfort certainly feature highly in many of my choices here, but nothing comes close to the Mercedes-Maybach S600 in terms of how many top features can be tweaked and tailored to cater for your individual needs.

It's fair to say the concept of a supercar that's roomy on the inside doesn't sit comfortably with every fan. In particular, this applies to models from manufacturers with a reputation for power, handling and performance. When Aston Martin announced what is effectively an estate version of the iconic DB9, it certainly divided opinion.

On paper, the Rapide S raises eyebrows. This four-door sports saloon is a not insignificant 16 ft long, but when you see it for real, any doubts that this is the right direction for Aston Martin simply disappear. In a word, it's gorgeous!

The design is the first thing to win you over. From the chassis upwards, the craftsmanship, aerodynamic engineering and aesthetics combine to dramatic effect. It doesn't feel like an extended DB9 but a grand tourer in its own right. The Rapide S looks sculpted rather than stretched while clearly coming from the Aston Martin stable. This is down to the refinement in body-shaping. It's solid but so beautifully rendered that it lifts the car into a class of its own. What's more, with rear-wheel drive coupled with a V12 engine capable of producing 552 bhp, the space it affords on the inside hasn't resulted in a compromise of power or performance.

Sure enough, when the Rapide S comes alive, it takes no prisoners. Squeezing the accelerator produces a deeply pleasing, intense noise and more than enough

ASTON MARTIN

RAPIDE S

torque to be sure that the car will deliver a thrilling drive. It'll see you from 0–62 mph in 4.4 seconds and can produce a top speed of 203 mph, which is hugely impressive on both counts. The Brembo brakes are reassuringly responsive and feel just right under your foot while the balance and adjustable suspension mean you can tailor the ride to suit your needs. Most notable of all is the fact that it doesn't handle like a four-door saloon. It feels like a GT even with passengers in the back seat or a lot of luggage in the boot, a deeply appealing prospect if you're taking a long journey.

From a driver's point of view, the sculpted seats and dashboard layout provides just the right balance between comfort and control. While it might be the case that leggy passengers find there's an art to squeezing into the car, once they're on board they'll find enough space in the back to settle comfortably and enjoy the performance car experience that Aston Martin never fails to deliver. The Rapide S is deceptively sure-footed for a vehicle of such length so if you're looking for a long-haul ride that still feels lithe and lots of fun, here is your dream car.

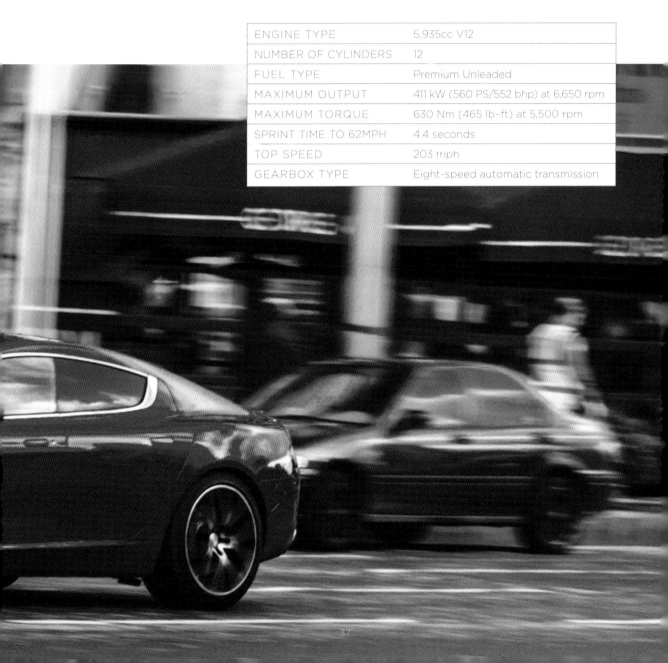

ENGINE TYPE	5,935cc V12
NUMBER OF CYLINDERS	12
FUEL TYPE	Premium Unleaded
MAXIMUM OUTPUT	411 kW (560 PS/552 bhp) at 6,650 rpm
MAXIMUM TORQUE	630 Nm (465 lb–ft) at 5,500 rpm
SPRINT TIME TO 62MPH	4.4 seconds
TOP SPEED	203 mph
GEARBOX TYPE	Eight-speed automatic transmission

What do the words 'family estate car' bring to mind? Comfort, space and reliability might be a popular requirement but that hardly sets the world on fire. While everyone needs to do grocery shopping, it's life-affirming to know your car has the potential to leave a cloud of dust behind it in the supermarket car park. Which brings me to the Audi RS 6. Yes, it provides everything you would come to expect from a four-door estate. It's a familiar shape, and yet the contouring and the 20-inch alloy wheels suggest something a little more... aggressive. Sure enough, when we move on to the performance stats, this is where the RS 6 departs from being a reassuringly dog-friendly kind of car and enters the sublime. Boasting an incendiary level of torque, it'll take you from 0–62 mph in well under 4 seconds, so you'd be wise not to let Fido stick his head out of the window in this ride.

The engine responsible for such mighty power potential is a Twin-Turbo, 4.0-litre V8. Anyone familiar with the Audi RS 6's previous incarnation will recognise the reduction in engine size compared with the 5.0-litre V10. But thanks to advances in design, material, engineering and aerodynamics, this actually feels better in terms of balance, handling and overall performance. In fact, once you're behind the wheel and feel the improved drive, it's fair to say this is one power estate for which a little less really does deliver a whole lot more. It picks up effortlessly and proves to be breathtakingly quick. For a moment, set aside the fact that it can fit your family or a bunch of mates inside. This is a phenomenally fast Audi. You can literally put your foot down and just watch the numbers rise.

As well as pace, the four-wheel drive RS6 handles beautifully. Much of this is down to the adaptive air-suspension system and Audi's fast and crisp gear transmission engineering. Combined with great weight distribution, intense grip and reassuringly rock-solid brakes, this is an estate car that surprisingly comes into its own on cornering. It means as well as pointing it in the direction of Europe's long, straight motorways, it'll deliver the goods on country lanes and winding passes. Inside, the quilted leather seats, quality dashboard, wheel and trim emphasise the car's sporting characteristics, which really don't feel out of place despite the size of the vehicle. Combining such performance scope with so much room in the back and the boot, in my view it really is the complete package for those big journeys.

ENGINE TYPE	3,993cc Twin-Turbo V8 TFSI
NUMBER OF CYLINDERS	8
FUEL TYPE	Premium Unleaded
MAXIMUM OUTPUT	412 kW (560 PS/553 bhp) at 5,700–6,600 rpm
MAXIMUM TORQUE	700 Nm (516 lb-ft) at 1,750–5,500 rpm
SPRINT TIME TO 62MPH	3.9 seconds
TOP SPEED	189 mph
GEARBOX TYPE	Eight-speed automatic transmission

AUDI

RS 6

GERMANY

SPEED AND PERFORMANCE

ROAD TRIP 03

GERMANY – SPEED AND PERFORMANCE

• • •

It's one thing to get behind the wheel of a supercar, but where can you go to bring it alive? When speed and performance are such critical components of the package, there can only be one place in Europe. I'm talking about a country famous for long stretches of public highway where you're not going to see the flashing lights of a squad car in your rear-view mirror for pushing the speedometer into triple figures.

Germany's autobahns have no blanket speed limit. Safety is still a priority, of course, just as it should be, but when traffic permits, it's possible to open up the throttle and experience the true potential of a supercar.

For this reason alone, I love travelling across Germany. The home of Audi, BMW, Mercedes-Benz and Porsche, this is a car-manufacturing country that shines like a beacon in the field of design, efficiency and technology. And when your stomach's rumbling after hours in the fast lane, you can't beat pulling into a service station and picking up the finest snack known to mankind on the move: the bratwurst. Throw in the Nürburgring motor-racing circuit for good measure, along with its iconic, incredibly demanding Nordschleife (north loop), and it's easy to see why drivers consider Germany to be something of a supercar heaven.

SHMEE150'S SELECTION

• • •

AUDI S8 PLUS

KOENIGSEGG ONE:1

PORSCHE 918 SPYDER

AUDI R8 V10 PLUS

BUGATTI VEYRON 16.4 GRAND SPORT VITESSE

AUDI
S8 PLUS

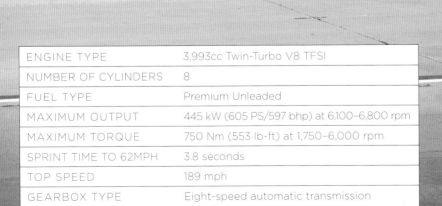

ENGINE TYPE	3,993cc Twin-Turbo V8 TFSI
NUMBER OF CYLINDERS	8
FUEL TYPE	Premium Unleaded
MAXIMUM OUTPUT	445 kW (605 PS/597 bhp) at 6,100–6,800 rpm
MAXIMUM TORQUE	750 Nm (553 lb-ft) at 1,750–6,000 rpm
SPRINT TIME TO 62MPH	3.8 seconds
TOP SPEED	189 mph
GEARBOX TYPE	Eight-speed automatic transmission

the autobahn, Audi's new S8 Plus transforms a long, straight drive into a hugely enjoyable experience. Above all, it's just so relaxing and manages to be both stately and ferociously swift. I clear the acceleration lane, find a good stretch and take it steadily towards 155 mph. The 750 Nm of torque is intense and the power seemingly infinite. My knuckles should turn white as I grip the steering wheel but the fact is I feel completely chilled out. For that, I have the car to thank.

Comfort is key here. The sports seats with contrasting red stitching are endlessly adjustable and designed to accommodate any driving style. As you might expect from Audi, the custom carbon-fibre interior is highly-specced and promises much to enjoy. Above all, however, the car is strikingly quiet, with reassuring carbon-ceramic brakes but an awful lot of go. I have to actually drop the gears and roll down the windows in order to hear the rumble and spit of the active sports exhaust. The Audi S8 Plus doesn't feel the need to make a lot of noise about its sheer power, speed and performance. It just pulls off the whole package with ease.

After some time on the road, I begin to think that this is a car that redefines the concept of cruising. It's incredibly fast, but never offers a sense of being on the limit, and for many drivers that's a perfect combination. Yes, there's a time and place for deploying all the skills you can muster behind the wheel to bring out the best in a supercar but sometimes a deeper pleasure comes from travelling at high speed with sheer grace, and the Audi S8 Plus delivers exactly that. This is a luxury machine, perfectly suited for long autobahn journeys in a way that leaves you feeling like the king of the road. The Audi S8 Plus is a beast trapped inside the body of a limo and presents an opportunity to take high-speed luxury driving to the next level.

This isn't just a supercar. Nor is it a hypercar. The Koenigsegg One:1 is a megacar. Not only that, it's a limited model. With a total of just seven cars manufactured, spotting one on the road isn't just a rarity – it's a life-enhancing moment.

The One:1 derives its name from achieving that magic – and often illusive – ratio of 1,361 PS metric-horsepower to 1,361 kg (3000.5 lb) mass. In effect, a 1:1 balance. This perfect power-to-weight set-up produces the equivalent of one megawatt in raw energy. That's estimated to be enough to light up 1,000 homes.

With such a huge amount of power at the driver's disposal, the One:1 demands respect but offers masses of enjoyment in return. A great deal of precision has gone into the aerodynamic design package and overall engineering to ensure the car's performance matches its sheer power.

This is a road car built for speed. Strapped into the cockpit, facing a trio of handsome digital displays behind the steering wheel, you feel like you're being offered complete control of a monster. The tachometer hits 3,000 revs and it's mind-boggling to think of the drive shaft rotating at such a rate. Feeling it, however, is another matter. The Koenigsegg One: 1 can reach 250 mph in just 20 seconds, with each upshift in gear promising even greater performance. The adrenalin rush is secondsond to none, as is the torque and handling, while it almost comes as a comfort to hit the carbon-ceramic brakes and feel this banshee on wheels subside from a scream to a throaty growl. Even by the standards of what you find on Germany's autobahns, this is one fast supercar, but speed is only one of its many impressive components. Designed and built in Sweden, the Koenigsegg One:1 is all about raw power, endless performance and engineering brilliance.

I've also been lucky enough to get a ride in a One:1 with a driver capable of bringing out the very best that the car has to offer. Ex-Formula 1 ace Adrian Sutil is the owner of the famous matte-black Koenigsegg Agera X, which tells you the man is a fan of the marque. It was joy to just hold on tight and witness Sutil overtake one supercar after another – from the Ferrari 458 Speciale to the Porsche 911 GT3 RS – as if they were standing still. If you're looking for raw power capable of obliterating the competition, the Koenigsegg One:1 is a winner from start to finish.

ENGINE TYPE	5,000cc Twin-Turbo V8
NUMBER OF CYLINDERS	8
FUEL TYPE	Premium Unleaded / E85 Biofuel
MAXIMUM OUTPUT	1,001 kW (1,361 PS/1,342 bhp) at 7,500 rpm
MAXIMUM TORQUE	1,371 Nm (1,011 lb-ft) at 6,000 rpm
SPRINT TIME TO 62MPH	2.8 seconds
TOP SPEED	280 mph
GEARBOX TYPE	Seven-speed automatic transmission

KOENIGSEGG

ONE:1

PORSCHE
918 SPYDER

This is the limited edition roadster that famously broke the production car world record for a lap time around the Nürburgring Nordschleife (6 min 57 seconds). For dipping under the seven-minute barrier to cover the challenging 12.8-mile north loop circuit in the Eifel mountains, the Porsche 918 Spyder has to feature as a selection in a country that celebrates high-end performance and astonishing speed.

With a 4.6-litre V8 and twin-electric motors, this is 887 bhp of elite motor engineering that can reach a top speed of 214 mph and go from 0–62 mph in just 2.6 seconds. In terms of design and engineering, Porsche have built upon their impeccable heritage to produce this standout hypercar.

The hybrid engine set-up works wonders. In E-mode, the electric motors produce a surge of power that's all the more remarkable for being completely silent. Switch to hybrid mode using a knurled rotary knob on the steering wheel and the all-familiar V8 roar kicks in to leave you in no doubt that this car has combined the very best of both old school and new technology.

With the exhaust tips right behind you, mounted on the rear deck, the noise is just insane. And it matches the car's speed capability. As the needle climbs, it sounds like the four horsemen of the Apocalypse are in hot pursuit and I love it. It's quite a wide car for an open-top, but the colossal roar from those pipes makes it feel just right. Travelling through tunnels, it really blows you away in every sense. But whatever the terrain, from the autobahn to a twisting mountain pass, the car affords a sense of complete control. The huge rear wing is a case in point. It's fully adjustable for optimum handling on challenging road secondstions or the simple pursuit of straight-line speed. Quite simply, this car is immense.

And with just 918 in production, it really is a question of catching this rare beauty when you can.

As I come to a standstill, as if to reinforce just how much power this car packs under the bonnet the engine shuts down automatically. With the top down, and birdsong on a gentle breeze, I'm left with a big smile on my face and the temptation to pinch myself to make sure I'm not dreaming.

ENGINE TYPE	4,593cc V8 + two hybrid synchronous motors
NUMBER OF CYLINDERS	8
FUEL TYPE	Premium Unleaded / Electric Charge
MAXIMUM OUTPUT	661 kW (899 PS/887 bhp)
MAXIMUM TORQUE	1,280 Nm (944 lb-ft)
SPRINT TIME TO 62MPH	2.6 seconds
TOP SPEED	214 mph (hybrid)
GEARBOX TYPE	Seven-speed automatic transmission

ENGINE TYPE	5,204cc V10
NUMBER OF CYLINDERS	10
FUEL TYPE	Premium Unleaded
MAXIMUM OUTPUT	449 kW (610 PS/602 bhp) at 8,250 rpm
MAXIMUM TORQUE	560 Nm (412 lb-ft) at 6,500 rpm
SPRINT TIME TO 62MPH	3.2 seconds
TOP SPEED	186 mph
GEARBOX TYPE	Seven-speed automatic transmission

AUDI

R8 V10 PLUS

B e prepared for this monster to roar. The Audi R8 V10 Plus has evolved through several generations which can be summed up as 'intense'. As a result, you can be confident that with a twist of the key this new edition will come alive with the visceral intensity of its predecessors – and possibly even exceed it.

Design-wise, the car is as aggressive as it sounds. From the wide, angular front grill and vents, the bodywork rises shark-like over the two-seater cockpit and then slopes back over the engine bay and carbon diffusers in one formidable package. As I guide the car onto the road, I'm presented with a digital display behind the wheel that can be customised to suit my needs. This is more than a toy. The state-of-the-art technology packed into the dashboard alone is a reflection of the R8's capacity to adapt to any driver's needs and enable them to bring out the best in the car. I opt for a big radial rev counter and put my foot down.

In many ways, this supercar reminds me of the Lamborghini Huracán. They share the same formidable 602 bhp and chassis set-up, but the Audi R8 Plus is a little less in your face. It's something I've come to admire from the marque but there's nothing understated about this car's sheer power. With one press of a button, I can open up the exhaust and truly appreciate that signature 5.2-litre V10 growl.

This isn't a car that's all noise and little substance. The Audi R8 V10 Plus comes into a class of its own on the open road. The seven-speed, dual-clutch transmission is lightning-fast and is a measure of Audi's dazzling ability to push the boundaries of performance. With electronically adjustable dampers, it's also capable of absorbing any bump or degradation in the road to deliver impeccable handling and an unmistakably sporty experience. It can also be quite playful. Engage the option to reduce traction and increase performance and the car becomes more sensitive. It's a nice choice when leaving the famous autobahn for Germany's winding country roads, and proves the car shines when it comes to handling as much as for its sheer velocity. Overall, in terms of fast, performance supercars, the Audi R8 V10 Plus provides enjoyment and excitement in equal measure. It really is a lot of fun and breathes racing DNA.

BUGATTI

VEYRON 16.4
GRAND SPORT
VITESSE

A s soon as I set eyes on this supercar, I knew I was in for a very special ride. The Bugatti Veyron 16.4 Grand Sport is arguably the most iconic street-legal sports roadster of the last decade – and certainly the fastest. The model I'm putting through its paces, with its distinct black and orange bodywork, is the Vitesse World Record Convertible (WRC). In earning this crown, it achieves a top speed of 254.04 mph. This is an insane figure! It's fair to say that I cannot wait to get behind the wheel.

I am well aware that this Bugatti is a beast, however. So, before I'm let loose on German roads that can only bring out the best in this mind-blowing performance car, I ride shotgun with Bugatti driver Andy Wallace. 'It's gonna be good,' says Andy when I strap myself into the bucket seat beside him. As he's just fired up the engine and the vehicle is already singing with power, I take this as an understatement. Even when he pulls away with gentle assurance, I'm already grinning from ear to ear.

We begin my Bugatti experience on an airfield track close to the Nürburgring. Andy positions the vehicle at one end of the runway secondstion and then brings us to a halt. I glance across at the driver's side. Andy is wearing mirror shades, but that doesn't hide the twinkle in his eye.

'A standing start?' I ask. 'That's one way to jump straight in.'

Andy grasps the wheel and encourages me to brace myself. We're looking down the barrel of the runway. The anticipation brings me out in goose bumps.

'It's almost like we're awaiting clearance to take off from the control tower,' he jokes.

Before I can respond, Andy hits the gas hammer. In a heartbeat, I feel as if I'm no longer in a supercar but strapped inside a rocket. The G-force plants the back of my head to the seat and the world outside becomes a blur. Three-quarters of the way down the runway, when Andy hits the brakes, the experience quite literally takes my breath away. I need a moment to recover my wits – but less than a secondsond to snap off the seatbelt when Andy invites me to take over.

Unlike Andy, I set off like a nervous kitten. Having seen – having felt – what this car can do, I am focused on easing myself into unleashing its full potential. I opt for automatic gearshift over manual (which can be overridden at any time using the paddles behind the wheel) and I cautiously pick up the pace. For a car that

ENGINE TYPE	7,993cc Quad-Turbo W16
NUMBER OF CYLINDERS	16
FUEL TYPE	Premium Unleaded
MAXIMUM OUTPUT	882 kW (1,200 PS/1,183 bhp) at 6,400 rpm
MAXIMUM TORQUE	1,500 Nm (1,106 lb-ft) at 3,000–5,000 rpm
SPRINT TIME TO 62MPH	2.6 seconds
TOP SPEED	254.04 mph
GEARBOX TYPE	Seven-speed automatic transmission

packs such performance power, I'm surprised at how quickly I feel comfortable. Some supercars demand time before you feel confident, but from the first corner onwards on what proves to be a technical, twisting track, I quickly feel in tune with the machine. It's clean and precise in every way. At one point, back on the runway, we hit 200 mph. In this car, it feels like the most natural thing in the world.

The Bugatti Veyron Grand Sport Vitesse WRC is, of course, a convertible. Andy suggests it's time to feel the wind in our hair and so we return to the airfield hangar to put the top down. Such is the vehicle's dedication to aerodynamic excellence, however, that I barely feel a strand of my hair moving. Even at over 180 mph Andy and I can still hear ourselves clearly.

I am mightily impressed and not a little thrilled when the time comes for me to hit the roads around the Nürburgring. Almost instantly I get a clear sense that this car offers as smooth and satisfying a drive on open country lanes as it does on a flat stretch of tarmac.

Ten years after its launch, the Bugatti Veyron Grand Sport Vitesse WRC still feels like the pinnacle of automotive engineering. This is a high point in my supercar dream that I'll never forget.

ALPINE

ADVENTURE

ROAD TRIP 04

ALPINE ADVENTURE

• • •

Around the world, every track and road is unique. Different conditions place a different combination of demands on both supercar and driver but arguably nothing is more challenging than Europe's mountain passes. From France and Austria to Switzerland and Italy, the Alpine states offer tight, twisting ribbons of tarmac, with constant shifts in elevation, undulation and gradient, all of which require focus and precision. There's no let up and such challenging passes demand that man and machine feel completely at one.

This high-altitude, high-octane secondstion of our tour is also about faith – in your abilities as much as the car – and a commitment to safety while pushing to the limit. The views might be spectacular, with majestic, snow-capped peaks and villages nestled in valleys under pure blue skies, but unless you're in the passenger seat there's no scope for sightseeing here. When you're behind the wheel of one of the world's most powerful supercars on narrow roads hugging steep mountain slopes, one wrong move won't just see you lose control. It could deliver you into the abyss.

For this reason alone, my selection for our alpine road trip is focused on agile sports cars and supercars with lightning-quick response times, superior handling and, of course, the power to deliver an unforgettable experience. In some ways, this road trip will prove to be hard work. Then again, when you're driving cars you love, the effort also brings a sense of exhilarating joy that's impossible to beat.

SHMEE150'S
SELECTION

• • •

PORSCHE CAYMAN GT4

McLAREN 570S

FERRARI 488 GTB

MERCEDES-AMG GT S

LAMBORGHINI HURACÁN
LP610-4

This isn't your everyday sports car. The Porsche Cayman GT4 is one of my prized Shmeemobiles. It's finished in a wonderful sapphire blue, and I'm very excited to feature it in my alpine road trip. Why? Because I'm as familiar with the vehicle's characteristics as much as its capabilities. I know just how it'll perform when let loose on roads that demand both skill from me as a driver and complete faith in the vehicle. You just cannot take on a mountain pass in a powerful performance car such as this with any sense of hesitation. You need to feel assured at all times, even on the limit, and the Porsche Cayman GT4 delivers that in every shape and form.

The GT4 is a special edition in the Cayman line, with a 3.8-litre Flat-6 engine taken from the 911 Carrera S, suspension components from the 911 GT3, a six-speed manual gearbox and numerous new aerodynamic features. This small and nimble but impressively hardcore sports car is a true driver's machine. From experience, I can truly say it ticks all of the required boxes.

This particular model features a number of exclusive options, from the adaptive sports seats to the silver seatbelts that match the stitching and trim around the black Alcantara and leather. It comes with a manual transmission for maximum involvement, which feels absolutely punch-perfect when grasped in my hand. On alpine roads, demanding frequent shifts, this can only mean one thing: an awful lot of focus and fun!

After a morning taking on scenic passes that corkscrew one way and the other, and with the ever-present barriers serving to remind me of the dramatic drops that lie on the other side, I can truly say the Porsche Cayman GT4 is a phenomenal car! It literally sticks to the tarmac wherever I choose to place it. The balance is incredible but the aerodynamics are in a class of their own. Much of this is down to the splitter at the front and the wing at the back, which provides just the right level of downforce to maximise performance without compromising control. Just be aware that in exiting corners with such intense power or in throwing on the brakes in preparation for a turn in, the forces you feel in the driver's seat can leave you short of breath. And I mean that in a very good way indeed!

In short, this incredible agile sports car has the capacity to provide you with the road car experience of a lifetime, but you have to earn the privilege. There's absolutely no sense of autopilot here. You have to learn how to harness the GT4's potential in the same way that a rider has to break a stallion – and I consider that to be a badge of honour. The Cayman range has always mightily impressed me and once you're up to speed (in every sense) the GT4 feels almost unsurpassable in terms of sheer driving pleasure. And on alpine roads that climb, twist and drop, there's no better place in the world to appreciate this rare combination of huge grip and traction, yet involving, intuitive handling.

ENGINE TYPE	3,800cc Flat-6
NUMBER OF CYLINDERS	6
FUEL TYPE	Premium Unleaded
MAXIMUM OUTPUT	283 kW (385 PS/380 bhp) at 7,400 rpm
MAXIMUM TORQUE	420 Nm (310 lb-ft) at 4,750–6,000 rpm
SPRINT TIME TO 62MPH	4.4 seconds
TOP SPEED	183 mph
GEARBOX TYPE	Six-speed manual transmission

PORSCHE
CAYMAN
GT4

McLAREN
570S

With big brothers in the shape of the P1 and 650S, this supercar comes with a high degree of expectation. Thrillingly, it exceeds on all counts. In particular, the most striking thing about the McLaren 570S is its sheer usability. Every aspect of this car has been designed with the driver in mind, which appeals to me as I contemplate threading the car along unforgiving stretches of mountain tarmac.

Climbing into McLaren's new sports car feels noticeably easier than its older stable-mates. The doors, which open with an upward tilt like the wings of Pegasus, provide improved entry room to slip behind the wheel. I'm now effectively inside a 75-kg carbon-fibre tub and it really does feel like it's built to connect the driver to the road.

The design is key here. As we set off at pace, marked by the growl of the Twin-Turbo V8, I'm aware that my sightline is directly level with the highest point of the front wheels. This is a very simple alignment but it provides me with absolute confidence in placing the car wherever I choose on the road. McLaren have seriously nailed the exact spot to place the driver in. This is such an essential aspect in handling a high-performance vehicle and many manufacturers would do well to follow their example. There's no shortage of power and it's very nicely delivered but, ultimately, I feel in complete control thanks to this visual reference afforded by the seating position alongside supreme handling in a well-balanced performance package.

The McLaren 570S offers three cars in one due to the multiple choices of powertrain mode (normal, sport and track), which offer very different and easily distinguishable experiences. To begin, I opt for normal, which provides me with an assured and seemingly effortless drive. With traction and stability control deployed, I can familiarise myself with the car, the road and the conditions. Once I'm happy, I opt for sport mode and that's when the car transforms. At once, I feel the limits of adhesion in the tyres and a snap-out from the back end as I seek to cling to the apex of a corner. It's a wake-up call and yet the car is so balanced that with quick wits you can swiftly bring it back into line.

To illustrate just how well this car serves the driver, a soft press of the gear paddle prepares the seven-speed transmission for a harder click to deploy the shift. The result: a blink-quick transition that proves vital on a snaking mountain pass. I have no doubt that track mode would place even more responsibility into my lap but that's for another road trip!

Overall, the McLaren 570S is an awesome machine. It's beautifully contoured both inside and out, combining carbon fibre with aluminium parts and it's available in a range of custom colours. My favourite has to be mantis green, which you wouldn't miss from the other side of the car park, but it's the handling capabilities that will actually turn most heads. Ultimately, this is irresistible for anyone looking for a performance road car that allows you to find just the right level of control.

ENGINE TYPE	3,799cc Twin-Turbo V8
NUMBER OF CYLINDERS	8
FUEL TYPE	Premium Unleaded
MAXIMUM OUTPUT	419 kW (570 PS/562 bhp) at 7,500 rpm
MAXIMUM TORQUE	600 Nm (443 lb-ft) at 5,000–6,500 rpm
SPRINT TIME TO 62MPH	3.2 seconds
TOP SPEED	204 mph
GEARBOX TYPE	Seven-speed automatic transmission

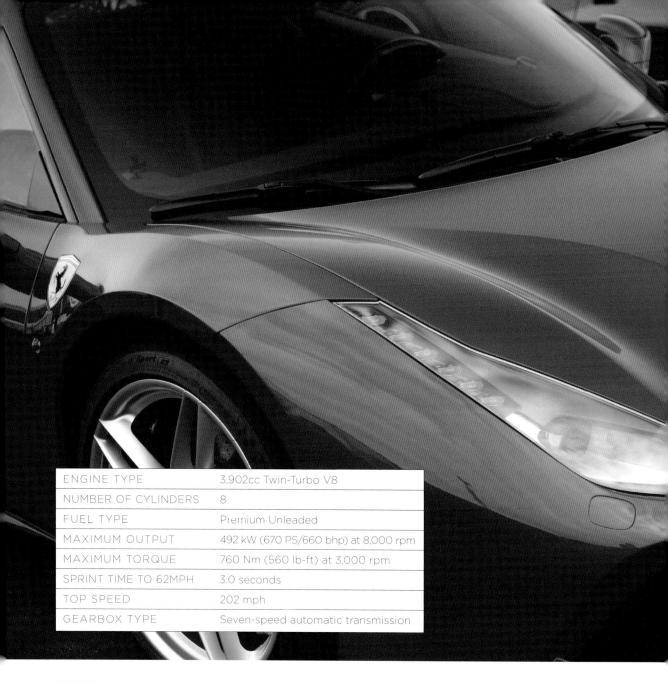

ENGINE TYPE	3,902cc Twin-Turbo V8
NUMBER OF CYLINDERS	8
FUEL TYPE	Premium Unleaded
MAXIMUM OUTPUT	492 kW (670 PS/660 bhp) at 8,000 rpm
MAXIMUM TORQUE	760 Nm (560 lb-ft) at 3,000 rpm
SPRINT TIME TO 62MPH	3.0 seconds
TOP SPEED	202 mph
GEARBOX TYPE	Seven-speed automatic transmission

This is the replacement for the much-admired 458 Italia, with a 3.9-litre Twin-Turbo V8 and I can tell you now that this vision on wheels doesn't disappoint. How can it be anything other than seriously impressive? We're talking about Ferrari here, after all.

Most notable of all is the departure from the naturally aspirated engine and a return to the brute force of a turbo. Straight away, this tells me that things are about to become a lot more powerful so it's reassuring to see the level of detail and refinement that's gone into the aerodynamic design. Every aspect of the bodywork has been optimised for airflow, from the split double vents at the rear and the active aerodynamics under the chassis to the engine cooling system. Even the door handles contribute to the package as they're both accessible from above to create subtle side fins. It's a small detail but contributes to the overall sense of a car that's optimised for balance and stability at speed. With my alpine roads in mind, I just knew that this was one

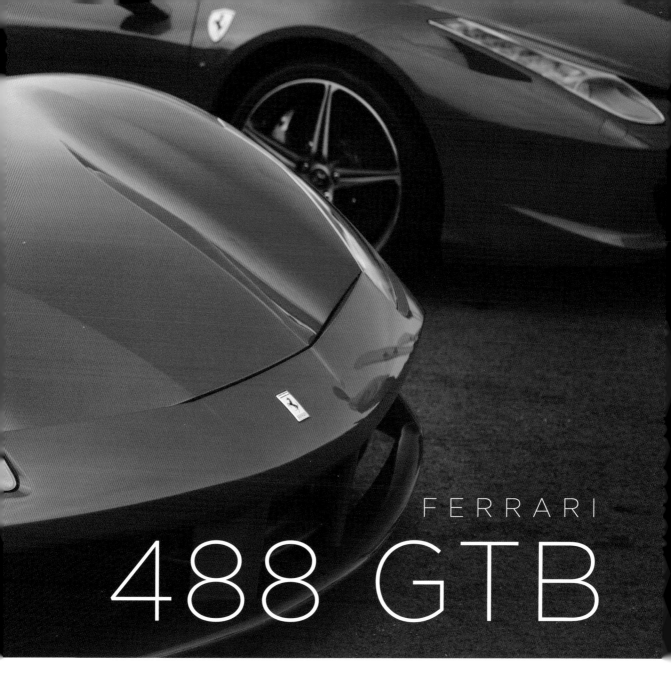

488 GTB

supercar with glue-like downforce to see me to the other side with a quickened heart rate and a beaming smile across my face.

Firing up the engine reminds you that this is a turbocharged beast. The guttural roar that assaults your ears will lead you to fear you're in for an untamed handful of a drive. In fact, quite the opposite is true and that makes for a unique combination. It's perfectly possible to step out around corners or even punch into a power slide, but it never feels like you're getting into

something from which you can't recover. The chassis makes an outstanding contribution here. It allows you to quickly feel in tune with the car and the road, providing confidence at every twist and turn, as well as realising the potential for a huge amount of fun. It's as quick as it is impressive and capable of nailing 0–62 mph in a mighty 3 seconds. Without a doubt, this Ferrari is a joy. It's a staggeringly nimble supercar; and perfect for those challenging mountain passes. It leaves you feeling on top of the world in every single way.

MERCEDES-
AMG GT S

H ere is a supercar jostling for space in a crowded market. The Aston Martin V8 Vantage and Porsche 911 are two of the leading competitors and yet one look at the Mercedes-AMG GT S suggests we may have a winner based on appearance alone. It really is a devilishly handsome beast, with a long bonnet and sleek bodywork that looks like it's been blasted into shape at speed.

And while it may be quick – boasting a 4.0-litre Twin-Turbo V8 that will take you from 0–62 mph in 3.8 seconds – it's the car's standout handling capabilities that demands it earns a stage in my alpine road trip.

With my foot on the brake, I hit the start/stop button. The car doesn't just come alive. It roars with such intensity that I imagine drivers of a meek disposition might switch it off and walk away. Even before I set off, I am left in no doubt that this Merc might well possess the kind of bite to match its bark. I choose from one of the driving modes to ease me in gently. Each one modifies many aspects of the car's handling and also allows me to input my own set-up with the aid of a neat screen interface. Toggling straight to race mode progressively opens the valve control and exhaust system while intensifying the revs. Imagine a Pamplona bull with fully adjustable anger settings and you begin to get a sense of just what this car can deliver when unleashed. Even in comfort mode, the simple act of pulling away produces a formidable growl.

ENGINE TYPE	3,982cc Twin-Turbo V8
NUMBER OF CYLINDERS	8
FUEL TYPE	Premium Unleaded
MAXIMUM OUTPUT	375 kW (510 PS/503 bhp) at 6,250 rpm
MAXIMUM TORQUE	650 Nm (480 lb-ft) at 1,750–4,750 rpm
SPRINT TIME TO 62MPH	3.8 seconds
TOP SPEED	193 mph
GEARBOX TYPE	Seven-speed automatic transmission

This is a supercar that sounds as good as it looks, but just how does it perform on our chosen road trip? Quite simply, the GT S delivers a thunderous driving experience. Yes, it's loud and you can expect to see both alpine goats and herders turn their heads but that intensity also translates to the car's behaviour on the road. You just know that this car wants to slide as you push into a corner but the exquisite balance and suspension set-up makes the high-octane experience feel exhilarating rather than terrifying.

Inside, you'll find a classic instrument cluster with a cutting-edge finish that is sure to impress. There is a radial speedometer and rev counter while the digital panel in the middle provides a menu of functions and settings at the touch of a button on the wheel. Behind, the hatchback space offers plenty of luggage room while the sleek strut brace reminds you this is a car that's begging to be put through its paces. In fact, the balance between tradition, technology and engineering feels just right throughout the vehicle. It's like AMG have taken the spirit of a muscle car, including the sheer romance of that experience and injected it into a modern age GT. It prowls and roars and looks like a million dollars, but above all it delivers a supreme driving experience on seriously unforgiving roads. That's an unbeatable combination, and I guarantee that when you finally come down the mountain you'll want to force the car into a cinematic 180° spin and do it all again.

LAMBORGHINI
HURACÁN
LP610-4

You might hear the new Huracán LP610-4 described as a 'baby' version of the mighty Lamborghini Aventador supercar, but don't let your guard down. This is no cute and cuddly outing from one of Europe's most distinctive marques. It might be more compact than the Aventador, but with a 5.2-litre V10 engine it's just as ferocious on every level – if not more so when it comes to taking on tight and twisting Alpine roads.

This Italian bull is instantly recognisable as belonging to the Lamborghini stable. It's a predatory, angular gladiator of a car that combines flat planes with

graceful curves. The vented rear engine cover suggests something seriously powerful lies inside, and it's enough to make your spine tingle with anticipation. With some supercars, it can be hard to know what you're driving once you're behind the wheel. The interior might be beautifully designed, but the manufacturer's identity is sometimes lost. Not so with the Huracán (pronounced Oo-rah-KANN). From the moment you settle into the sportiva seats, Lamborghini's iconic hexagonal design becomes apparent with subtle but pleasing effect. It's present in the shape of the new dash system, which boasts a 12-inch LCD display, the air vents and even the wing mirrors. It makes you keenly aware that you're behind the wheel of a Lambo, which is just as it should be when you bring it to life.

The sound of the engine is mightily pleasing on several levels. It's a tight, intense and powerful roar, but the resonant pops and crackles leave you in no doubt that this car will pack a punch. On setting off, I find the seven-speed, double-clutch gearbox is fantastically quick on the shifts. It provides an immediate sense of response and control, which is exactly what you need on mountain roads. Move from 'Strada' into 'Sport' mode using the ANIMA mode selector, which translates as 'soul' but sounds like an Italian corporate bank, and you'll feel how nicely balanced the car is. There are no nasty surprises

awaiting you, but neither is there anything to make you laugh out loud. The steering is tight, allowing you to fully explore the traction and grip of the four-wheel-drive system. On tarmac ribbons that can twist and turn like a rollercoaster at times, this provides me with the kind of confidence that comes close to performance-car nirvana.

And the noise! It's impressive even at a standstill with my foot on the gas hammer, but at speed the Huracán lives up to its fearsome-sounding name. From the other side of the range, it must sound like the thunderstorm from hell is set to break loose. When I push the car into 'Corsa' – the most ferocious mode – and shift up a gear using the manual paddles, it feels like I've just been kicked in the back of the seat by a stallion. It is, by far and away, the most exhilarating way from getting to A to B with an Alpine range in between.

In wider supercars like the Aventador, I'd spend a great deal of time skipping heartbeats on negotiating narrow stretches of road. In the more compact and agile Huracán, those potentially paint-scraping moments become an opportunity to let loose, and I love it. Ultimately, this is a very cool, full-throated supercar that's quite possibly capable of causing an avalanche and effortlessly outrunning it at the same time. When it comes to my Alpine road trip, Lamborghini have just earned a prime place in the pack.

ENGINE TYPE	5,204cc V10
NUMBER OF CYLINDERS	10
FUEL TYPE	Premium Unleaded
MAXIMUM OUTPUT	449 kW (610 PS/602 bhp) at 8,250 rpm
MAXIMUM TORQUE	560 Nm (412 lb-ft) at 6,500 rpm
SPRINT TIME TO 62MPH	3.2 seconds
TOP SPEED	202 mph
GEARBOX TYPE	Seven-speed automatic transmission

ROAD TRIP 05

DESIGNS ON
ITALY

DESIGNS ON ITALY

• • •

I've come to what might just be Europe's spiritual home of motoring. This is a country brimming with passion, colour, taste, style, attitude, integrity and a capacity to celebrate road power, driving skill and speed like no one else.

I'm talking, of course, about Italy.

You only have to consider some of the iconic manufacturers to appreciate just what the country has contributed to performance car culture – on the road and in motorsport. From Ferrari, of course, and Alfa Romeo to Pagani and Lamborghini, they have created marques celebrated across the world.

As well as the cars, and celebrated motor racing circuits such as Modena, Mugello, Imola and Monza, Italy has been host to one of the best-known open road endurance races in history, the Mille Miglia. Running annually for 30 years from 1927 (except in 1939 and 1941-6), the race was estimated to draw up to 5 million spectators along the length of the route, a phenomenal number and a measure of just how central the car had become to Italy's rich and varied culture.

Then there are the road trips to consider. Italy is home to some of the finest routes in the world, embracing the challenge of the Alps, the rolling countryside of Tuscany and the elemental, breathtaking scenery from Basilicata to Sardinia. Rome, Florence and Milan might be notorious for gridlocked streets, but this is no hardship when you're behind the wheel of a supercar. If anything, in a country where people truly appreciate the good things in life, you and your ride become an attraction… and that can be just as much fun as hitting the open road.

So, for this trip, I'm looking for supercars with qualities that make them quintessentially Italian. Performance power is top of my list, but I want to feel some history behind the wheel, along with the intensity and panache that makes this country and its motor racing pedigree so unique.

SHMEE150'S SELECTION

· · ·

FERRARI LAFERRARI

PAGANI ZONDA S

LAMBORGHINI MIURA SV

SCG 003 S

ALFA ROMEO 8C COMPETIZIONE

FERRARI F40

FERRARI
LAFERRARI

The LaFerrari is described as a hybrid hypercar. The first part of this power package comes in the shape of a mighty 6.3-litre V12 engine in the back that is good for 789 bhp. Then we have the Kinetic Energy Recovery System (KERS), which has become a familiar feature in Formula 1. By calling upon power harnessed under braking, this helps to deliver an additional 161 bhp, bringing the total to an insane 950 bhp. Just on the performance figures alone, you know the LaFerrari is going to be a very special ride indeed.

This is a car that looks like it's capable of taking you to a speed of 217 mph. Design-wise, it's sleek, futuristic and predatory. Catch this approaching in your rear-view mirror and instinctively you'll prepare to be swallowed whole. Behind the wheel in the car's Italian homeland, you can expect bystanders to simply drop their groceries and gawp or just burst into a round of applause. It is an astonishing machine.

The carbon-fibre tub interior feels very much like that of a race car. The seats are actually bolted to the chassis, which means adjusting the steering wheel and pedals for comfort. In a car dedicated to performance, the dash is nicely minimal. In fact, all the menu controls you need are largely packed into the display that sits alongside the radial rev counter. To complete the sense that you're on the grid awaiting lights out, there's a launch control selector, track telemetry function and even a fire extinguisher strapped to the passenger floor well.

Quite simply, from the moment you pull down the wing door, it's clear you're inside the maw of a monster, but one that's awaiting your command. Given this, you might think that merely brushing the accelerator would deliver you directly over the nearest cliff edge. In reality, the LaFerrari is surprisingly easy to handle. It can produce the mother of all kicks on the upshift and never fails to remind you of its power potential, but I guarantee it'll leave you feeling exhilarated.

If you can set aside the incredible speed, which is frankly impossible, the handling is delightfully deft. This makes it attractive for any kind of road layout, and a must for my Italian outing. With a seven-speed, dual-clutch, rear-wheel drive and a million-pound price tag, the slightest twitch or slide out of a corner can cause your knuckles to tighten around the wheel, but this is not a car that's waiting to outfox the driver. Despite the lightning velocity potential, it's built to drive like a dream, while inviting more attraction than a magnetic bullet shot through a storm of iron filings. I absolutely love it.

ENGINE TYPE	6,262cc V12 + HY-KERS unit
NUMBER OF CYLINDERS	12
FUEL TYPE	Premium Unleaded / Electric Charge
MAXIMUM OUTPUT	708 kW (963 PS/950 bhp)
MAXIMUM TORQUE	>900 Nm (>663 lb-ft)
SPRINT TIME TO 62MPH	<3.0 seconds
TOP SPEED	217 mph
GEARBOX TYPE	Seven-speed automatic transmission

PAGANI
ZONDA S

S ome supercars look like they've been delivered from another planet. The Pagani Zonda S, on the other hand, has quite clearly been built by humans – and the level of artistry, verve and engineering tells you that these humans are Italian. Even so, you'd be forgiven for thinking it might've been conceived in the future and then sent back in time to show us what we can look forward to in years to come. That's how unique the Zonda S is to me.

It also sounds like no other supercar. When fired up, the exhaust produces an opera of noise. You just know that once you're harnessed into the driver's seat, there awaits an experience like no other.

Pagani first introduced us to this car of tomorrow in 1999 with a limited production run that ended in 2011. Even now, the Zonda remains streets ahead of the competition in terms of its combination of design, sound track and sheer performance power. Every edition packs a V12 engine capable of unleashing quite astonishing ferocity. The 760 spec, often considered to be the ultimate track-focused spec, almost refuses to behave nicely. It kicks, spits, snarls, slides and roars and moves so rapidly that blinking is often not an option. But in the right hands, with assured control, it becomes a work of automotive art.

With a sky-high price tag and the fact that it's so quick it's easy to miss, the Zonda is a marvel in the supercar world. Like a shooting star, the car creates an air of wonder and awe. It's an unforgettable machine, inside and out, and a tour through Pagani's home country is a truly fitting way to celebrate what mankind can do at the forefront of automotive technology. With the naturally aspirated Zonda featuring in my selection – a car that absolutely nails the concept of throttle response – this drive is guaranteed to thrill from start to finish.

ENGINE TYPE	7,291cc V12
NUMBER OF CYLINDERS	12
FUEL TYPE	Premium Unleaded
MAXIMUM OUTPUT	408 kW (555 PS/547 bhp) at 5,900 rpm
MAXIMUM TORQUE	750 Nm (553 lb-ft) at 4,050 rpm
SPRINT TIME TO 62MPH	3.6 seconds
TOP SPEED	214 mph
GEARBOX TYPE	Six-speed manual transmission

Describing how a supercar sounds at full rev can be testing at times. Yes, the engine might bellow, roar and scream but in my opinion it's the exhaust note that shows true character. So, for my next selection, I've opted for a dream machine that will leave Italian car lovers in no doubt about its identity from a mile away. I'm talking about the Lamborghini Miura, often considered to be of the first Italian supercar.

This is a supercar that sounds like it runs on high-octane fuel and honey. It's full-throated, sonorous and sweet and I cannot hear enough of it. What's more, the Miura also happens to be one of the most beautiful sports cars Lamborghini have ever made. Its long bonnet yields to a wraparound windscreen, graceful, sweeping body curves and a tight, compact rear. Produced between 1966 and 1973 and the first car to break the 200 km/h (124.3 mph) barrier, this two-seater, rear-wheel drive and mid-engined marvel is widely considered to be a design classic. It pretty much set the standard for the modern performance car and looks just as relevant today as it did all those years ago.

Founder and supercar visionary Ferruccio Lamborghini loved the Miura so much he considered it to be his go-to car. So, too did Frank Sinatra, which goes some way to show how achingly cool it really is.

On the road, the V12 engine delivers volume as much as muscle, but the car's precise tuning makes that noise as delightful as birdsong. You sit low in the cockpit, looking out along the length of the bonnet and genuinely feel as if you're in the presence of performance car perfection. Each transmission shift locks in like a puzzle piece, which requires a little care, but this can only remind you that Lamborghini's top engineers first drew up the blueprint for the Miura over 40 years ago.

Car design continues to evolve, as does engineering and advances in speed, power, handling and performance, but the Miura is a reminder that once in a blue moon a perfect storm of creativity occurs. It brings together the very best of every automotive discipline available at the time and produces a supercar that just cannot be improved upon. Whether you're parked at the piazza, drawing looks of astonishment and admiration or sweeping along roads between vineyards, the Lamborghini Miura and its faster brother the Miura SV with 380 bhp on tap are a work of art on wheels and sums up the Italian spirit in every way.

ENGINE TYPE	3,929cc V12
NUMBER OF CYLINDERS	12
FUEL TYPE	Premium Unleaded
MAXIMUM OUTPUT	283 kW (385 PS/380 bhp) at 7,700 rpm
MAXIMUM TORQUE	388 Nm (286 lb-ft) at 5,500 rpm
SPRINT TIME TO 62MPH	6.7 seconds
TOP SPEED	171 mph
GEARBOX TYPE	Five-speed manual transmission

LAMBORGHINI

MIURA SV

SCG 003 S

Every season in motor racing, a newcomer joins the big names on the grid and immediately shakes up the running order. The same can be said for supercar manufacturers. In fact, I'm so impressed by the power, grace and styling of one such recent entrant that I've selected it for my Italian road trip. The creator may not be Italian but each vehicle has been built by craftsmen just outside Turin. Collectively, they have embraced the qualities of Italian car building and their passions shines through.

As the number suggests, the Scuderia Cameron Glickenhaus SCG 003 S is just the third outing for the company owned by former movie director, Jim Glickenhaus, but it's ahead of the pack in many different ways. This is a game-changing machine, inspired by Le Mans Prototype racer technology and available in two editions. The track version has already posted a time of 6 minutes 42 seconds around the Nürburgring, beating the standard Pagani Zonda R by five seconds. If that isn't enough to stop you dead in your tracks, consider the fact that the second version has been rendered entirely road legal.

I was lucky enough to be introduced to the car by Jim himself. He explained the philosophy behind his vision: 'We wanted to make a car that sculpted the air around it to the rear wing in the most efficient way,' he told me, sweeping a hand along his incredible creation before detailing some of the challenges his engineers overcame in meeting road regulations.

In order to maximise the aerodynamic efficiency of the wing mirrors, for example – by placing them strikingly high – the car is able to feature dashboard cameras that provide the driver with the complete picture. It's an innovation that works wonders, and adds to the sense that you're in control of a jet fighter on wheels. As Jim took me around the car, highlighting a rear wing that's more expensive than some entire supercars and emphasising

how the movement of air has guided and informed every square millimetre of its design, I know just where the SCG 003 S will be truly appreciated… in a country that recognises the importance of form and function working closely together. In melding both of these features into one entity, Jim Glickenhaus has created an American dream of a car with a distinctly Italian sensibility. There really is nothing else like it.

Not only does the SCG 003 S look incredible, set to become an established time-sheet topper on the track, but the road version's V6 engine promises to deliver an equally intense road experience. It's a supercar that you need to see to believe, and on this road trip you can be sure that your passengers will be quick to take it to their hearts as if it were their own.

ENGINE TYPE	Twin-Turbo V6
NUMBER OF CYLINDERS	6
FUEL TYPE	Premium Unleaded
GEARBOX TYPE	Six-speed automatic transmission

There's no denying that Alfa Romeo know how to make a stunning car. For design alone, the Alfa Romeo 8C Competizione would win all the prizes. This two-seater sports coupé from the mid- to late-90s is about long, sleek curves and classic, refined styling and proves just perfect for my Italian excursion. It really is as visually pleasing as a priceless vase. The only difference is that vases don't contain a V8 engine delivering thunderbolts of power to the rear wheels – they're not even mobile, in fact – which makes the car a much better investment.

Climbing into a bucket seat which is both firm and deliciously low-slung, I'm presented with a carbon fibre-trimmed interior that's striking for its simplicity. In many ways, this sums up the car's heightened sophistication. Like Italian cuisine, you'll find only the essential ingredients in this automotive dish and it tastes all the better as a result. All the controls you need are present and correct, with no extraneous buttons and switches destined to gather dust. Less means so much more here and it works. The 8C Competizione is simply a masterpiece – not just in appearance but also on the road and that's where sheer driving pleasure becomes a serious business.

Admittedly, the car's handling can be a challenge in comparison to its contemporaries but then the 8C is all about passion. From the sound track to the stunning design lines – and of course the Alfa Romeo badge – what you have here is a driving experience that isn't purely focused on performance. Sometimes, you just want to feel like you're behind the wheel of a moving work of art and in this car you get exactly that.

With 480 Nm of torque, 0–62 mph in 4.2 seconds and a top speed of 181 mph, the 8C provides all the power you need for an Italian road trip of a lifetime. Whether you choose the coupé or roadster model, you're looking at a beauty with a beast under the bonnet. From failing to keep a low profile in the city to kicking up a storm cross-country, I can't think of a better combination. Unfortunately, Alfa Romeo made just a small production run, with every car snapped up by drivers who know a good investment when they see it – not just financially but in terms of sheer motoring enjoyment.

ENGINE TYPE	4,691cc V8
NUMBER OF CYLINDERS	8
FUEL TYPE	Premium Unleaded
MAXIMUM OUTPUT	331 kW (450 PS/444 bhp) at 7,000 rpm
MAXIMUM TORQUE	480 Nm (354 lb-ft) at 4,750 rpm
SPRINT TIME TO 62MPH	4.2 seconds
TOP SPEED	181 mph
GEARBOX TYPE	Six-speed automatic transmission

ALFA ROMEO 8C

COMPETIZIONE

FERRARI

F40

When you're passionate about supercars one of the greatest pleasures lies in seeing how they have evolved over the years. Technology has played a huge role here. Today, as we move towards the reality of a self-driving car, it's already possible to let the modern high-performance vehicle take the sweat out of much of the driving. This can only add to the thrill of slipping behind the wheel of a vintage supercar. It might mean more work in harnessing the car's true potential on the road but that's no bad thing at all. Especially not when it comes to my final automotive star under the spotlight for my Italian road trip. We're back with Ferrari once more, who book-end my selection, with the incomparable F40.

Much like the Alfa Romeo 8C, this is a car that melds form and power. It's a supercar stripped of any pretence or preening. Despite being a product of the late 80s, the F40 is no celebration of material wealth. If you're looking for bells and whistles on this car, you'll be disappointed. Everything about the F40 is dedicated to the pursuit of speed and automotive excellence. Quite simply, if it doesn't help the car to go faster, balance, handle better, adhere to the road or boost your sense of unfettered joy and exhilaration behind the wheel, then the guys at Maranello deemed it surplus to requirements. But we're not talking about assists here – there are none. If you want to bring out

the best in this supercar, then it's down to you to up your game considerably.

Even today behind the wheel of the F40 you can be thankful for such single-minded vision and commitment. While the competition squabbled over ways to attract attention in an increasingly crowded market, Ferrari arguably went back to basics. So there isn't much to note in taking you around the interior but consider that to be a really good thing. Want to crack open the windows? Use the handle. The dashboard is never going to be a distraction when you're on the road – but that's just how it should be. The result of such a stripped-down approach, as I twist the ignition key to revel in the V8 Twin-Turbo growl, puts Ferrari in pole position.

In short, the F40 is one of the finest supercars ever to grace the road. It looks phenomenal, with the kind of wing you might compare to an old-school F1 car. That's also how it drives. This is a handful, make no mistake, but it offers such mighty, unvarnished power that it leaves today's assist-laden cars looking like they might as well be fitted with stabilisers. And this is the big draw here. The F40 demands respect and once you've given it, the car begins to yield and deliver on every level. It really is fast and furious, but above all there is precision engineering at work here – and in the right hands, it dazzles.

ENGINE TYPE	2,936cc Twin-Turbo V8
NUMBER OF CYLINDERS	8
FUEL TYPE	Premium Unleaded
MAXIMUM OUTPUT	352 kW (478 PS/472 bhp) at 7,000 rpm
MAXIMUM TORQUE	577 Nm (425 lb-ft) at 4,000 rpm
SPRINT TIME TO 62MPH	3.9 seconds
TOP SPEED	201 mph
GEARBOX TYPE	Five-speed manual transmission

ROAD TRIP 06

MONACO,
BABY!

MONACO, BABY!

• • •

The pocket-sized principality on the French Riviera is a paradise for the supercar enthusiast. Monaco may not be big, occupying less than a square mile in front of the French Alpes-Maritimes, but it's a playground for the world's rich and famous. This is evident in the kind of boutiques, casinos, hotels and restaurants that grace the boulevards as well as the super-yachts berthed in the harbour, and it's also reflected in the vehicles you'll find there.

In Monaco, the streets are narrow, often with hairpin corners and they can be steep in places. They're also dripping with style, affluence, culture and prestige. What's more, thanks to the Grand Prix that takes place here every year – one that is considered to be the jewel in the F1 crown – many of the circuit's landmarks have become icons of motor racing, from Casino Square to Beau Rivage, La Rascasse and the long, languorous tunnel that swoops around to the harbour. In essence, what we have here is a celebration of streets, tight turns and grand hotels.

A short climb out of the principality takes you onto steep and winding hillside passes that can take your breath away. There is nothing like stopping at the roadside overlooking the Mediterranean and the glittering little city below to feel like you've arrived. And if your ride happens to be a Ferrari or a Bugatti then you can safely say to yourself that it doesn't get much better than this.

So, what am I looking for on a road trip here? Prestige and luxury driving feature high up on my list, of course. But in addition to cars that make you feel like a millionaire and which are begging to be seen, I want to be sure that I can make the most of those wonderful hills. From cruising in a compact but exclusive urban environment to taking on hillside climbs with confidence – that's a broad set of requirements. With this in mind I've spent a lot of time selecting the ideal cars that ensure you make the most of your visit from the moment you sweep into town.

SHMEE150'S SELECTION

...

ROLLS-ROYCE DAWN

FERRARI 250 GTO

RENAULT TWIZY

FERRARI 458 SPECIALE

MERCEDES-BENZ 300 SL GULLWING

ROLLS-ROYCE
DAWN

M y first entrant comes from a manufacturer considered to be the grandfather of prestige driving. The Rolls-Royce Dawn follows in the tyre treads of the hugely admired Wraith. As a convertible, it's thought of as an informal extension of the family, designed and engineered for slow, stately boulevard driving. It's definitely a car to be seen in and to be enjoyed as both a driver and a passenger.

In short, this is exactly the kind of luxury cabriolet for a road trip to Monaco, if you want to become the talk of the town. When the Dawn purrs in, you can't help but look and metaphorically doff your cap. It simply oozes class and prestige in every conceivable way.

The Dawn has a new front end which is nevertheless not a major departure from the flat, square nose we all recognise – and the Spirit of Ecstasy is inevitably mounted in place at the prow – but the tight and focused LED headlights give the overall design an impressive feeling of concentration. The bonnet is as long and sleek as ever, but it's the rear three-quarters that truly defines the car. Here, the lines swell over the shoulder and then taper away while the compressed soft top reminds me of

a hot rod. It's a scintillating design that manages to be both regal and seriously exciting at the same time.

Inside the Dawn beats a 6.6-litre Twin-Turbo V12 heart that will take you from 0–62 mph in 4.9 seconds. Where Rolls-Royce stand apart from the competition is in how that power is delivered. You're unlikely to see a roller put down rubber on the tarmac, but when this one moves away there is majesty in its power and poise. With an eight-speed transmission it's capable of swift, smooth upshifts. This delivers a seamless driving experience that is as close as you can imagine to riding a magic carpet. What's more, it's satellite-aided – the car reads the road ahead and anticipates exactly which gear you need, while a night-vision system can pick up on heat signatures in the road. Even by todays standards, these are deeply impressive features.

Inside a Rolls-Royce convertible it's only natural that the first thing to try out is the roof. On pressing the button, you'd be forgiven for thinking that nothing is happening. That's because the mechanism has been engineered so exquisitely that it's all but silent. Then the Mediterranean sun floods the interior. You glance up and see swimming-pool blue skies as the soft top concertinas and folds into the rear bodywork. It's at this moment that the Dawn shows off its true glory. The car takes on an entirely new look.

Passengers in the rear seats will be tempted to give a royal wave, such is the voluptuous styling and gravitas the car affords. Naturally, there's a great deal of wood finishing which looks incredible, but this time Rolls-Royce has truly embraced technology. Having taken care of a smooth ride and road safety, the gadgetry extends to the kind of on-board entertainment system you'd expect to find in a playboy's apartment. It really is a stunning addition to an already incomparable pedigree and a strikingly seductive motor car fit for a king.

ENGINE TYPE	6,592cc Twin-Turbo V12
NUMBER OF CYLINDERS	12
FUEL TYPE	Premium Unleaded
MAXIMUM OUTPUT	420 kW (571 PS/563 bhp) at 5,250–6,000 rpm
MAXIMUM TORQUE	780 Nm (575 lb-ft) at 1,500–5,000 rpm
SPRINT TIME TO 62MPH	4.9 seconds
TOP SPEED	155 mph (governed)
GEARBOX TYPE	Eight-speed automatic transmission

L et's be honest, driving this two-seater racing GT through the streets of Monaco is likely to bring the entire principality to a standstill. It isn't just that the car is an outstandingly beautiful work of Italian engineering and artistry. Nor will you draw crowds solely on its rarity (just 39 produced between 1962 and 1964) or because it's widely considered to be Ferrari's finest work. The fact is that the 250 GTO is highly collectable and valued in the region of a staggering £15–20 million. On that basis alone, what we have here is a showstopper.

This is a supercar that only Ferrari could've created. It's sleek, refined, elegant and sexy but possesses the poise and confidence of a race car produced to take on the likes of the Shelby Cobra and Jaguar E-Type. Impeccable curves draw the eye from the long bonnet to a compact back end and rear spoiler that immediately tell you the 250 GTO is built for speed and stability. The side vents stand out on this car like claw marks and serve to remind you that aerodynamics are central in delivering the optimum driving package. With a 3.0-litre V12 engine producing 296 bhp and a five-gear transmission, this is a car that can dance around the race track with blistering pace and perfect balance. Even at a standstill, pitted or parked, it's just so good to look at that people will come flocking.

On climbing into the cockpit, you find very little to take your eye off the road. The interior has been stripped back to cater for the racer, with cloth seats and basic vents. The dash is so basic that it doesn't even sport a speedometer! But then, in a car this sublime, the sole focus really should be on the pleasure and exhilaration of the ride and nothing else. In effect, the only thing worth measuring here is your enjoyment behind the wheel and, frankly, that's just off the scale.

The 250 GTO is all about driving purity and it's here that you begin to appreciate its astonishing value. Yes, some might say it's just a car, but this one captures the essence of what it means to put four wheels on the road. And in Monaco we have what I would consider to be the finest backdrop for a car of this pedigree. Whether you're cruising the boulevards or threading around the hills behind the principality, the Ferrari 250 GTO will deliver a drive that most can only dream of.

ENGINE TYPE	2,953cc V12
NUMBER OF CYLINDERS	12
FUEL TYPE	Premium Unleaded
MAXIMUM OUTPUT	221 kW (300 PS/296 bhp) at 7,400 rpm
TOP SPEED	174 mph
GEARBOX TYPE	Five-speed manual transmission

FERRARI
250 GTO

HOTEL DE PARIS

RENAULT

TWIZY

O K, so there are bound to be some raised eyebrows for this entry. When it comes to making the cut, we're looking at power, performance, design and handling, right? Well, yes, and I've judged this two-seater electric quadricycle on just that criteria. Even the entry-level Urban 45, with a top speed of 28 mph, will give Ferrari and Bugatti a run for their money on this Monaco trip. In fact, if challenged to get from A to B through the choked city streets, the chances are the Twizy would take the chequered flag nine times out of ten.

At just under 7.5 ft in length and available with or without side windows, some might suggest that Renault's all-electric urban runabout isn't even a car, but on design alone I would beg to differ. This little electric vehicle (EV) reinvents modern transportation in traffic-heavy environments, while featuring a cutting-edge combination of design and engineering. I assure you that behind the wheel – and with the wind whistling around the cockpit – 28 mph feels three times faster. And when every other car in Monaco is crawling, despite their price tags and capabilities, the Twizy really is the only way to go.

It can also shift, attaining that blistering (in Monaco traffic) top speed in a little over 4 seconds. That's quite a lot of torque from an emission-free, battery-charged, 17 bhp engine. Enough to wipe the smirk from any driver's face when they see you slipping nimbly through an otherwise gridlocked Monaco street. Even on stretches where the traffic flows, the Twizy is quite capable of keeping up with the pack.

In many ways, Renault have produced a scooter for people who don't feel comfortable on two wheels but appreciate efficiency in movement, form and function. The body incorporates roll bars and a harness to strap you into the seat and, while the dash offers little more than a motorbike, it fulfils every function you need. In a bustling, built-up environment, the Twizy comes into its own. What's more, and this is critical, you never feel as if people are looking at you for all the wrong reasons. The bodywork calls upon bold curves and offers a pleasing ride height that literally puts you head and shoulders above the traffic. Ultimately, if you're considering a trip in or near a busy city such as Monaco and you have a long list of people to meet and places to see, the Renault Twizy will swiftly become your go-to vehicle in the garage. And when you consider the contenders you choose to leave behind, that makes it a superior car by any standard.

ENGINE TYPE	Electric Motor
NUMBER OF CYLINDERS	0
FUEL TYPE	Electric Charge
MAXIMUM OUTPUT	13 kW (18 PS/17 bhp)
MAXIMUM TORQUE	57 Nm (42 lb-ft)
SPRINT TIME TO 62MPH	n/a
TOP SPEED	50 mph for Urban 80 model
GEARBOX TYPE	Single-gear automatic transmission

FERRARI
458 SPECIALE

This is a car that seriously calls upon Ferrari's extensive experience in Formula 1 engineering technology. Following on from the standard 458 Italia and the 430 Scuderia, you only have to hear the 4.5-litre engine's dominating roar to register the serious innovation and brutal performance potential. Its forerunner, the 430 Scuderia, was no slouch, but the 458 Speciale takes the marque's mid-engine V8s to an entirely new level. It isn't just louder but it also has an increased engine capacity and a jaw-dropping 597 bhp. The insane power is framed by an intuitive intelligence. Combined, it delivers a drive that can only bring out the best in your abilities.

What we're talking about here is arguably the standout feature in the car's suite of technological advances: the sideslip angle control system. This is state-of-the-art, algorithm-driven software that assesses any turn you take in real time to ensure you're hitting the apex. It's incredibly subtle, ensuring true grip, stability and precision power delivery on exiting any corner. The system encourages you to refine and optimise your driving skills and rewards you with an unforgettable, exquisite experience.

Without question, this is a focused supercar and not just in terms of what's under the bonnet. It's beautifully sculpted, as you would expect from Ferrari, while weight reduction and downforce efficiency inform the aerodynamic design. The front air flaps that open up at 105 mph to minimise drag and then adjust automatically as you continue to push. This keeps the car planted and creates the sense that nothing can hold you back. There's certainly little inside to weigh you down, which is in keeping with the pursuit of driving purity. Jump behind the wheel and it makes a lot of sense. All of a sudden, in a cockpit focused solely on connecting you to the car and the road, the lack of satnav and stereo feels liberating. These things just exist to distract you, right?

So, as a showcase for design and engineering, the 458 Speciale ticks all the right boxes for a trip to Monaco. It's an immensely powerful package making full use of technology and looks simply stunning in both the original and convertible editions. In this exclusive principality, where Ferraris are as easy to spot as black cabs in London, the 458 Speciale is guaranteed to make its presence known. You can cruise through the boulevards and revel in the response or put it to the test in the hills and marvel at the performance.

ENGINE TYPE	4,497cc V8
NUMBER OF CYLINDERS	8
FUEL TYPE	Premium Unleaded
MAXIMUM OUTPUT	445 kW (605 PS/597 bhp) at 9,000 rpm
MAXIMUM TORQUE	540 Nm (398 lb-ft) at 6,000 rpm
SPRINT TIME TO 62MPH	3.0 seconds
TOP SPEED	202 mph
GEARBOX TYPE	Seven-speed automatic transmission

MERCEDES-BENZ
300 SL GULLWING

My supercar selection for Monaco wouldn't be complete without a classic. For a road trip through a city that appreciates the finer things in life, such a car has to feel just as it did when first manufactured – timeless. That's a tall order, because history isn't always kind when it comes to car design. Innovation is a vital part of the evolution process, for better and sometimes worse, but every now and then comes a model that is a perfect representation of the ultimate in design and engineering of the age. This is embodied in my next choice: the Mercedes-Benz 300 SL Gullwing, the world's first supercar.

The car looked like no other when it was designed in the 1950s and much of this was down to the doors. The gullwing design might have entered the popular imagination thanks to the DeLorean DMC-12's star turn in the *Back to the Future* movie trilogy of the late 80s and early 90s, but Mercedes-Benz had been the true pioneers more than 30 years earlier.

Produced in 1954, this two-seater sports coupé featured doors that hinged from the roof. On opening up, much like a seagull spreading its wings, it looked like no other car. It was such a leap in design evolution that the term 'car' really didn't do it justice. The Mercedes-Benz 300 SL Gullwing was a sensation then and continues to be so today.

But it isn't just the doors that make this supercar special or the fact that it was the first to feature a fuel-injection system designed to appeal to the motor-racing aficionado. The sheer beauty of its design, alongside that performance power drawn from the manufacturer's Grand Prix racing heritage, ensured the 300 SL would become an instant smash. What makes it all the more amazing is the fact that the car's popularity never waned. If anything, it has simply strengthened.

So, what do we have here, apart from one fine-looking coupé? Underneath the long, elegantly sculpted bonnet, you find a 3.0-litre engine that produces a top speed of

160 mph, making it the fastest road-legal car of its time. The 300 SL really did push boundaries of both design and performance and inspires nothing but admiration from both driver and supercar fan. Every line that defines the car is poetry in motion. The flat front wheel hoods and rocket-like side vents contribute to the overall sense of design and engineering perfection. It's the kind of star turn you'd expect from Italian automotive maestros because it's packed with passion and aerodynamic artistry as much as precision performance engineering. In some ways, the arrival of the Mercedes-Benz 300 SL arguably helped to reintroduce Germany to the world post-war as a country capable of great heart and soul.

It feels like a privilege to slip behind the wheel. Straight away, you're rewarded by a sense of heritage, not just in the design but in the roar on firing up the engine. As for your experience on the road, that first squeal on cornering is sure to bring a smile to your face. While the handling is strikingly idiosyncratic, the car packs considerable punch that requires focus and respect at all times. And yet, even by today's standards, the Mercedes-Benz 300 SL can deliver a thrill with the same intensity as it did over 60 years ago and not just for the driver. Even before you've brought this landmark vehicle to a halt and spread the doors wide open, it's sure to attract an audience who appreciate its legacy.

ENGINE TYPE	2,996cc Inline-6
NUMBER OF CYLINDERS	6
FUEL TYPE	Premium Unleaded
MAXIMUM OUTPUT	158 kW (215 PS/212 bhp) at 5,800 rpm
MAXIMUM TORQUE	274 Nm (202 lb-ft) at 4,600 rpm
SPRINT TIME TO 62MPH	7.2 seconds
TOP SPEED	160 mph
GEARBOX TYPE	Four-speed manual transmission

DUBAI
DREAM

ROAD TRIP 07

DUBAI DREAM

• • •

There's one place in the world where you're never farther than a block away from a supercar: Dubai. Located on the Persian Gulf coast, this glittering city is one of seven emirates within the United Arab Emirates. Skyscrapers tower high into the Arabian sky, twinkling in the desert sun. Meanwhile, in the broad avenues and boulevards below you'll find a paradise for shopping, socialising and showing off behind the wheel of hugely powerful performance vehicles. The parade, very much a celebration of the dream machine, is part of the fabric of this city.

In Dubai, even the police drive luxury vehicles. It isn't uncommon to hear sirens blaring and then turning to see the department's Lamborghini Aventador screaming past. With everything from a Bentley Continental GT, Ford Mustang GT and a Mercedes-Benz SLS AMG to a Bugatti Veyron wrapped in the force's white and dark green colour combination, it's fair to say that spotting a patrol car here isn't just reassuring but a joy to behold.

This is a city that positively encourages vehicle one-upmanship. It can be a spectator sport and has resulted in huge advances in customisation as supercar owners try to steal the glory from their rivals. Bodywork wraps are commonplace, as are upgrades and refinements to exhausts and engines, aerodynamics and suspension systems. Then there are the select few with multiple supercars in their collection. These have been put together with care and attention, as if assembling works of art. Many collectors have cars that share trademark colour schemes and spotting them on the streets is extra-satisfying.

In deciding on my own selection for this road trip, my focus is on supercars with unique qualities. If you want to stand out here, you need to be driving a high-performance vehicle like nothing else. Yes, customising your wheels can help to set you apart from the pack, but underneath there has to be pedigree, power and that magic ingredient to ensure you're the cream of the crop… desirability.

KOENIGSEGG REGERA

LAMBORGHINI VENENO

MERCEDES-BENZ G 63 AMG

PAGANI HUAYRA

MERCEDES-BENZ SLR McLAREN STIRLING MOSS

MASERATI MC12

KOENIGSEGG
REGERA

This is one good-looking megacar, although considering its many outstanding qualities, such a description doesn't really do it justice. In short, the Koenigsegg Regera is a miracle on four wheels. It redefines concepts of design and engineering and is also blisteringly powerful. And you can consider that to be the ultimate understatement. To give you some idea of the stats, we should disregard the standard 0–62 mph measurements (2.8 seconds for the record) and head straight to the headline figures. The Koenigsegg Regera will take you from a standing start to almost 250 mph in just under 20 seconds.

So, what's responsible for such a jaw-dropping feat? Let's begin with the fact that this incredible megacar is a petrol-electric hybrid. As well as a 5.0-litre Twin-Turbo V8, it boasts not one but three electric motors while doing away with a standard transmission system. With no gear-shifting required, Koenigsegg have found a way to shorten the journey the available power needs to travel from the engine in order to turn the rear wheels. The result is a shake-up in car evolution that other manufacturers can only hope to follow. We're talking about an increased delivery in torque and performance that, in effect, creates a road-hugging missile. All credit to the owner Christian

von Koenigsegg and his team of engineers, therefore, for conjuring up a chassis and body that harness such mighty potential and makes the Regera completely drivable.

Fittingly, the car looks like a rocket. The wraparound window defines and informs the ultra-streamlined bodywork design. It's sleek, low-slung and dominated at the back by a top-mounted rear wing that uses airflow to deploy it, thus reducing the size and weight of its hydraulics. In a car that redefines power delivery, Koenigsegg have ensured that aerodynamic efficiency clearly guides every atom in its construction.

Let's be clear, even in a city where the supercar is commonplace, the Regera will draw attention and admiration in equal measure. Behind the wheel, you get a vivid sense that you're driving bleeding-edge technology. The dashboard is pleasingly simple, elegant and stylish, underlining Koenigsegg's Swedish roots and yet packs a comprehensive suite of controls into a central touchscreen panel. After dark, the high-intensity LED headlamp beams light up the road ahead for almost 1,150 feet. Not only does this ensure that you're seen as well as heard, but it provides vital illumination for the driver when piloting a car capable of swift, steady and gearless acceleration. It really is a case of strapping in, grasping the wheel of the Regera and preparing for a ride like no other, and I'm delighted to feature Koenigsegg's masterpiece in my choice of supercars for this road trip through the Arabian city of gold.

ENGINE TYPE	5,000cc Twin-Turbo V8 + three electric motors
NUMBER OF CYLINDERS	8
FUEL TYPE	Premium Unleaded / E85 Biofuel / Electric Charge
MAXIMUM OUTPUT	1,103 kW (1,500 PS/1,480 bhp)
MAXIMUM TORQUE	>2,000 Nm (>1,475 lb-ft)
SPRINT TIME TO 62MPH	2.8 seconds
TOP SPEED	248 mph
GEARBOX TYPE	Koenigsegg Direct Drive (KDD)

Here's a supercar for those who considered the Aventador LP700-4 to be Lamborghini's pinnacle in car design and performance. In presenting the Veneno, despite a production run of just four coupés and nine roadsters, the company has made a strong statement. It's basically a message to the motoring world that the company will never stop pushing boundaries in the pursuit of perfection.

Named after an Italian fighting bull celebrated for its strength and aggression, the Veneno undoubtedly lives up to its namesake on appearance alone. It's a prowling, muscular design that borders on the futuristic while calling upon classic Lamborghini characteristics. The tapering front wedge makes it immediately identifiable, as does the angular scoop of the overall shape. The fact that I can see the spirit of 1970's Urraco here as much as the Aventador just goes to show what a strong sense of identity the company can call upon. Within the Veneno's carbon-fibre monocoque is an interior also based on the Aventador but subtly refined – and I love it.

Even in Dubai, a Lambo will always turn heads and earn whistles of appreciation. To drive a model as rare as the Veneno through the sun-baked avenues and boulevards will ensure some supercar lovers stop dead in their tracks.

While the design earns much-deserved attention as a showcase of organic advances, the Veneno boasts the same 6.5-litre V12 engine as the Aventador. Unwilling to sit on their laurels, however, Lamborghini have squeezed the performance capability to deliver 740 bhp. With your foot down, this will take the coupé to an incredible maximum speed of 221 mph. To put things in perspective, that's a shade quicker than the Ferrari LaFerrari. Such stats combine with the predatory design – and the absence of a roof on the roadster – to make it very clear that this is not a supercar for the faint-hearted. Like riding a bull, you're going to need courage and confidence to master this mighty machine, but once you have, it will reward you with the ultimate thrill.

With 20-in racing wheels at the front and 22-in at the back and a seven-speed, single-clutch automated ISR (independent shifting rod) transmission, the Lamborghini Veneno is a race car rendered road legal. It's built to break records as much as earn respect and admiration and I have no doubt it'll make a clean sweep on both counts. This is a supercar that needs to be seen in the wild to be truly appreciated and what better stage than a city that celebrates the very best in automotive power, speed, design and performance? The Veneno might be an incredibly rare beast but when you unleash this Italian bull on a street run through Dubai, you will command the entire city's attention.

ENGINE TYPE	6,498cc V12
NUMBER OF CYLINDERS	12
FUEL TYPE	Premium Unleaded
MAXIMUM OUTPUT	552 kW (750 PS/740 bhp) at 8,500 rpm
MAXIMUM TORQUE	690 Nm (509 lb-ft) at 5,500 rpm
SPRINT TIME TO 62MPH	2.9 seconds
TOP SPEED	221 mph
GEARBOX TYPE	Seven-speed automatic transmission

LAMBORGHINI
VENENO

MERCEDES-BENZ
G 63 AMG

Sometimes in Dubai you need to think differently to stand out. In an urban jungle where the streets are host to sinuous, prowling and tiger-like supercars, the sight of an SUV is akin to spotting a rhino: an equally magnificent creature and one that deserves respect for many reasons. The key is to select an SUV that can also be considered a supercar and in the G 63 AMG, Mercedes-Benz has unleashed a beast that sits comfortably in both categories. That the emirate's ruler, Sheikh Mohammed bin Rashid Al Maktoum, is a proud owner, speaks volumes about its appeal.

It may lack the graceful curves and aerodynamics you would come to expect from a high-performance vehicle, but then the G-Class comes with a history that can only command respect. Known in Germany as the Geländewagen, which translates as 'cross-country vehicle' this model belongs to a class of 4x4 with seriously workmanlike qualities. It's tough, robust and more than capable of handling the desert dunes outside Dubai just as it is the muddy fields back home. But just because it can deal with a speed bump – unlike many supercars – exactly what is it that propels the G 63 into the same league?

The answer lies in the performance power, handling and high degree of luxury that await you behind the wheel.

Take the engine, which is a Twin-Turbo 5.5-litre V8. Potentially, that's a huge amount of power to call upon

ENGINE TYPE	5,461cc Twin-Turbo V8
NUMBER OF CYLINDERS	8
FUEL TYPE	Premium Unleaded
MAXIMUM OUTPUT	420 kW (571 PS/563 bhp) at 5,500 rpm
MAXIMUM TORQUE	760 Nm (560 lb-ft) at 1,750–5,000 rpm
SPRINT TIME TO 62MPH	5.4 seconds
TOP SPEED	143 mph
GEARBOX TYPE	Seven-speed automatic transmission

and our G-class representative under the spotlight doesn't disappoint. Granted it might weigh 2.5 tonnes, but with 563 bhp at your disposal – plus a seven-speed automatic transmission – you can take it from 0–62 mph in 5.4 seconds flat. This really is a sight to behold, especially in a city like Dubai, but it isn't the only reason why the G 63 makes the selection for my road trip.

The bodywork is pleasingly rugged on the eye but with a sports exhaust and 20-in alloy wheels, you just know it's capable of outperforming your standard countryside 4x4. The interior is perhaps the greatest indicator that you're in the lap of luxury. Mercedes-Benz has reworked the dashboard to provide finesse alongside function. The full-colour screen that takes

centre stage gives you a host of controls, along with several driving options that enable you to squeeze the very best performance from the vehicle across a range of conditions. It feels very contemporary on the inside, a design that works as the perfect counterpoint to the classic but artfully refined exterior. I can best describe the driving experience as 'upright' but this is no bad thing. It's incredibly comfortable, providing maximum visibility for both you and the supercar spotters on the streets and absolute confidence across all terrains. Combined with the sheer power on offer, this incarnation of the Mercedes-Benz classic G-class series is without doubt the toughest, smartest and most desirable SUV on the block.

ENGINE TYPE	5,980cc Twin-Turbo V12
NUMBER OF CYLINDERS	12
FUEL TYPE	Premium Unleaded
MAXIMUM OUTPUT	537 kW (730 PS/720 bhp) at 5,800 rpm
MAXIMUM TORQUE	1,000 Nm (738 lb-ft) at 2,250–4,500 rpm
SPRINT TIME TO 62MPH	3.0 seconds
TOP SPEED	230 mph
GEARBOX TYPE	Seven-speed automatic transmission

If I say that this hypercar comes from the makers of the Zonda, you'll be forgiven for thinking it can't possibly be any better. Ever since Pagani released their now iconic rear-wheel drive dream machine in 1999, the Zonda has come to be considered as one of the finest high-performance vehicles the world has ever seen. For some supercar disciples, it can never be bettered. Personally, I think keeping an open mind provides the potential for surprise and joy when a contender comes along and threatens to steal the crown. It's healthy and encourages car manufacturers to keep pushing at the limits of performance and design. But when the contender in question comes from the same manufacturer, you have to credit their confidence while recognising that what you're witnessing is a classic lineage in the making.

I am seriously excited about introducing the Huayra to the streets of Dubai. It's instantly recognisable as a Pagani stablemate but even on an audible level it serves up a different experience. Powered by a 6.0-litre Twin-Turbo V12, the Huayra delivers 720 bhp, an eye-popping 1,100 Nm torque, an incandescent top speed of 230 mph and the kind of crackles and bangs that were absent from the naturally aspirated Zonda. Many prefer the purity of sound delivered by the Zonda, but it really is down to your own preference.

Both cars are the brainchild of the Argentine founder of Pagani Automobili, Horacio Pagani, who is justifiably

PAGANI

HUAYRA

considered to be one of the greatest living performance car creators. While the Huayra's body design references the raised haunches and tapering spine of the Zonda, it features stunning gullwing doors and plenty of new aerodynamic lines. You'll also find front and rear flaps that operate automatically for optimum downforce delivery on cornering, accelerating and braking. It's a truly beautiful sight to behold, complemented by an exquisitely crafted interior. If you know the Zonda's capabilities, it promises a breathtaking drive.

But no matter how familiar you might be with the Huayra's predecessor, nothing can prepare you for the moment that you put this new incarnation to the test. The thump in the back on changing gears is guaranteed to wake up any driver foolish enough to think that this car can take care of itself. The culmination of efficiencies in weight and power delivery together with the new active aerodynamic design is responsible for the Huayra's astonishing performance. With the potential to leave smoking tyre tracks in your wake, the car demands great discipline in focus. At the same time, it handles intuitively, with impeccable balance and advanced assists, allowing you to maximise your skills with confidence. In essence, this state-of-the-art hypercar demonstrates how technology can be harnessed to push performance to new levels. Just thinking about unleashing this car's immense potential thrills me, and I know you'll feel the same way just as soon as you jump behind the wheel.

In order to compete in the FIA GT Championship, manufacturers must have produced at least 25 road-legal editions of the car they are entering. In returning to the championship after 37 years, Maserati did just that by introducing the MC12 to the world. In considering the reasons for its existence, you already know that this supercar is going to be a cut above the rest.

It's also massive, at almost 16.5 ft, a length that provides a whole lot more to appreciate. The simple fact is that Maserati have produced an incredibly pleasing car to behold. It really does look like it should be sweeping under a chequered flag, which makes the prospect of taking one through Dubai even more delicious.

The main thing to consider here is the history of the car. Strip away the sleek, artfully sculpted race design from the roof fin down to the side vents and the massive rear wing and what you'll find underneath is the carbon composite chassis and V12 drivetrain of a Ferrari Enzo. What Maserati have done here is take the foundations of a tried, tested and respected supercar and created an entirely new entity. This is no prancing horse by another name, however. The MC12 offers a completely different appearance and driving experience and calls upon seismic levels of power and performance.

It packs a mid-mounted V12 6.0-litre engine, which might serve up a little less power than the Enzo but you get a more refined and efficient bang for your buck in terms of stability, balance and control, which is often a winning formula out on the track. It's a joy to get behind the wheel – with fixed seats and harness a nod to the car's racing counterpart – and bring it to life. The sound is monstrous. You can feel each rev through every fibre of your body, which promises only good things as you pull out under the desert sunshine and prepare to stop traffic when you shift through the gears.

From an observer's point of view, there is little to distinguish the road and race versions. The MC12 really does look like it has no place on the streets, which is what will earn so much attention, and yet it handles like a dream, whether you're cruising through boulevards or watching the speedometer climb on desert roads.

With a top speed of 205 mph and the ability to take you from 0–62 mph in just 3.8 seconds, there's ample power on show here as you put the MC12 through its paces. Going by appearance alone, it effectively looks like one very fast fish out of water. In fact, just thinking about how people will react when they spot that predatory roof fin scything through the traffic, is enough for me to feature the Maserati MC12 on my Dubai road trip. In a city where the supercar is a familiar fixture, this is your chance to show that this Maserati is capable of shaking up the scene.

ENGINE TYPE	5,998cc V12
NUMBER OF CYLINDERS	12
FUEL TYPE	Premium Unleaded
MAXIMUM OUTPUT	463 kW (630 PS/620 bhp) at 7,500 rpm
MAXIMUM TORQUE	652 Nm (481 lb-ft) at 5,500 rpm
SPRINT TIME TO 62MPH	3.8 seconds
TOP SPEED	205 mph
GEARBOX TYPE	Six-speed automatic transmission

MASERATI

MC12

DESERT

ROAD TRIP 08

OUTRUN

DESERT OUTRUN

• • •

Whenever you have been hanging out in a city with a supercar, lighting up the streets and soaking up the attention, there comes a time when the urge to hit the open road becomes irresistible. With so much performance power at your disposal, it's only natural that you should want to unleash that sense of speed and freedom.

Having spent time in Dubai, our next road trip will take us out onto the desert roads that skirt the Persian Gulf. I have an epic route, defined by crystal blue coastal waters, endless plains of drifting sand and, of course, the occasional camel. We're off to Bahrain this time, taking in Qatar along the way and skirting the Saudi border. This is where you truly feel a sense of adventure. In the constant presence of a molten sun by day and galaxies of stars at night, you'll feel as connected to the universe as you will to the road and so it's vital that we choose the kind of vehicles that befit this experience.

I'm looking to make my choice here based on the concept of excellence. From purity of design, to performance and engineering, these have to be cars that are considered by many to be unrivalled in their field. Some might beg to differ, which can only give rise to healthy debate. So, I'm more than happy to kick off the conversation by introducing you to a set of cars that I would happily put to the test on the long haul from the seven emirates to one of the finest island jewels of the Gulf.

...

MERCEDES-BENZ G 63 AMG 6x6

W MOTORS LYKAN HYPERSPORT

LAMBORGHINI AVENTADOR LP700-4

ASTON MARTIN ONE-77

PORSCHE CARRERA GT

MERCEDES-BENZ
G 63 AMG
6x6

U pon setting off on an adventure of this magnitude, where the outside temperature needle can climb towards 38°C at times, you need to feel sure that you've chosen the right tool for the task. A car that simply looks the part won't cut it. We're going to need a set of wheels that will be guaranteed to deliver us to our destination, which means power and comfort in equal measure. So, to begin, there can only be one vehicle to lead the way and it's a beast on six wheels.

Should we feel the need to cut corners on this journey, the Mercedes-Benz G 63 AMG 6x6 would have no problem tackling the desert dunes. At close to 4 tonnes in weight, it's effectively a high-performance pick-up truck that handles magnificently. The first thing to acknowledge is the secondsond rear axle. The four 37-in wheels on the back of this brute don't just go round and round, they combine with the two at the front to produce enough muscle and clambering capabilities to negotiate the most challenging terrains, as commissioned for use by the Australian army.

ENGINE TYPE	5,461cc Twin-Turbo V8
NUMBER OF CYLINDERS	8
FUEL TYPE	Premium Unleaded
MAXIMUM OUTPUT	400 kW (544 PS/537 bhp) at 5,500 rpm
MAXIMUM TORQUE	760 Nm (560 lb-ft) at 1,750–5,000 rpm
SPRINT TIME TO 62MPH	7.8 seconds
TOP SPEED	100 mph (governed)
GEARBOX TYPE	Seven-speed automatic transmission

Once you move past the wheels, the next thing to admire about the G 63 AMG 6x6 is its sheer size. It requires a step up to climb in, but once you're behind the wheel there's no doubt that you'll feel like the king of the desert road. The fact that the 6x6 is fitted with comfy leather seats should tell you a great deal about what's in store. Where other vehicles might quickly get bogged down, this monster vehicle simply burns across the desert landscape. Like a ship on a storm-tossed sea, it climbs, lifts and drops down dunes with ease and this is where you really appreciate the extra back wheels.

In what could potentially be a stomach-churning ride, the 6x6 set-up, along with immense suspension, simply soaks up the troughs and ridges while the handling proves assured at all times. It's worth noting that this road trip also includes more conventional road surfaces. On the long, flat stretches through the desert you can look forward to a smooth drive in what feels like a cocoon of a cabin. There's no need to stop, get out and work up a sweat inflating your tyres to accommodate the harder surface. Thanks to the suite of controls on offer inside the cabin, it can all done without leaving your seat.

It's easy to see why the Australian military were drawn to the G 63 AMG 6x6. A session behind the wheel will help you to appreciate why it's just as effective for civilian use if you're planning on heading off the beaten track. With a 5.5-litre Twin-Turbo V8 under the bonnet providing a mighty 537 bhp, 760 Nm torque and the ability to conquer 0–62 mph in under 8 seconds, this is the SUV that will take on any challenge and deservedly earn its stripes.

There's no need to go off-road with this next pick for our desert outrun. Even if you have to take the long route, the Lykan HyperSport produces such astonishing speed that you'll still get there in no time.

Fittingly, this is a hypercar from an Arabian manufacturer, UAE-based W Motors. It's a hugely impressive debut for the region. The Lykan HyperSport comes in at a staggering £2.1 million but brings with it a 3.7-litre, Twin-Turbo flat-6 engine. This can produce an intense top speed of 240 mph. Underpinned by incredible acceleration potential, taking you from 0–62 mph in just 2.8 seconds, there's no doubt that this new kid on the desert block is set to leave its rivals in a cloud of sand.

So, apart from rip-roaring speed and power, what else do you get for your money? Firstly, it's designed to look as priceless as it does predatory. Hypercars are at the forefront of technological innovation and here this extends to the aerodynamic design as much as power delivery. Visually, the fierce, angular body shape and scissor doors look like the car takes its cue from the Terminator as much as Italian performance car heritage. And, visually, it works. It looks like it can get the job done and very possibly bend the space-time continuum in the process.

As befits a multi-million-dollar mean machine, the Lykan HyperSport's LED headlights are embedded with hundreds of 15-carat diamonds. You might not notice without being told, but it's guaranteed they'll dazzle. The exclusivity extends to the production run – W Motors plan to make just seven units, which makes the prospect of jumping behind the wheel for our desert outrun even sweeter.

The sense of futuristic opulence continues inside the car. Settling into the gold-stitched seats, the first thing you'll notice is that the dash looks unconventional with controls projected into the cockpit space as a 3D floating hologram. Once you've got your head around this mindblowing concept and take the car out onto the desert road, it actually makes a lot of sense. Controls are activated through simple swiping gestures, making it less necessary to take your eyes off the road to search out a more conventional button or switch. And in a hypercar this powerful, you're going to need eyes on stalks.

Firing up the engine makes your heartbeat quicken. The engine growl is arrestingly deep, with a whistling top note confirming you're inside a vehicle that marries science fiction with automotive fact. Naturally, many people will question whether any car is worth such an extraordinary price tag, although the Lykan HyperSport does come emblazoned with enough precious stones to fill a bank vault as well as an elite concierge service and a unique Cyrus Klepcys watch. It's impossible to put a figure on the elation that arises from hurtling at the speed on offer towards a vanishing point where the desert road meets the sky.

ENGINE TYPE	3,746cc Twin-Turbo Flat-6
NUMBER OF CYLINDERS	6
FUEL TYPE	Premium Unleaded
MAXIMUM OUTPUT	582 kW (790 PS/780 bhp) at 7,100 rpm
MAXIMUM TORQUE	960 Nm (708 lb-ft) at 4,000 rpm
SPRINT TIME TO 62MPH	2.8 seconds
TOP SPEED	240 mph
GEARBOX TYPE	Six-speed manual transmission or Seven-speed automatic transmission

W MOTORS LYKAN

HYPERSP

LAMBORGHINI
AVENTADOR
LP700-4

ENGINE TYPE	6,498cc V12
NUMBER OF CYLINDERS	12
FUEL TYPE	Premium Unleaded
MAXIMUM OUTPUT	515 kW (700 PS/690 bhp) at 8,250 rpm
MAXIMUM TORQUE	690 Nm (509 lb-ft) at 5,500 rpm
SPRINT TIME TO 62MPH	2.9 seconds
TOP SPEED	217 mph
GEARBOX TYPE	Seven-speed automatic transmission

Here is a supercar that charmed and bewitched the critics. Launched in 2011, the Lamborghini Aventador LP700-4 was accorded accolades and praise that rivals could only dream about. It's a masterpiece of design and engineering that clearly benefited from the Italian manufacturer's impeccable reputation. More importantly, it boasts a level of performance power and handling that are just begging you to jump in and explore for yourself – and what better stage to do so than the open desert road?

So, what makes this supercar just so good? For starters, the low-slung, flat and geometrical design harks back to the glory days of the Lamborghini Countach. In production from 1974 to 1990, the Countach earned a reputation for being a wild, fearsome drive that only rewarded the brave. It's the stuff of legend and you can't help wondering what you've let yourself in for on climbing into the Aventador.

In terms of power, the car is a sandstorm generator, with a 6.5-litre V12 engine producing a 0–62 mph sprint in 2.9 seconds and a top speed of 217 mph. There's no doubting the punch on squeezing the accelerator and that's when the Aventador defies all further comparisons – not just with the Countach but with contemporary supercars in the same class.

Make no mistake, we're talking about a ferocious driving experience here. The car can feel a little heavy as you throw it into a corner, but there's more than enough power to bring it out without compromise. On an aerodynamic level, the deep side-scoops and adjustable rear spoiler make absolute sense at speed, and you'll get there with a single-clutch gearbox that's so brutal, every shift delivers a kick that takes your breath away.

The V12 engine is located in the bay directly behind the cockpit. Naturally it's incredibly loud, but majestic in tone and a fitting reflection of the passion Lamborghini have invested in this car. It spits pure venom through the exhaust, snarls and crackles like wildfire and will sound like music to your ears as you focus on the desert road ahead. In many ways, this is a car that matches the epic landscape. Such wide open spaces provide no distraction from the Italian bull in your control. It's extreme, elemental and as dominating as the Arabian sun.

ASTON MARTIN
ONE-77

I n the interest of transparency, I have to confess a long-standing admiration for this car. I'm so in love with the ultra-rare, exquisite Aston Martin One-77 – named after the number of units in existence (77) – that I run a website tracking the location of as many as I can around the globe.

Introduced to the world at the 2008 Paris Motor Show, the Aston Martin One-77 fast became one of the most coveted hypercars on the planet, despite a price tag in excess of £1.2 million. It's an outstandingly handsome two-door coupé, featuring aluminium bodywork that's been sculpted and shaped by hand to absolute perfection. Just one look tells you it's an Aston, but this has a leaner, meaner edge than, say, the DB9. Everything is just a little tighter in the haunches, as if this beast is preparing to strike.

With a naturally aspirated 7.3-litre V12 engine providing 750 bhp and 750 Nm in torque, the power and performance potential is immense. The One-77 will take you from 0–60 mph in just 3.7 seconds and can unleash a top speed in excess of 220 mph. Then there's the noise. Many supercars know how to make their presence known on the ears, but Aston Martin nail it here. It isn't just about volume but a savagery of tone that has persuaded many wealthy supercar lovers to add this model to their collection.

The One-77 is without a doubt among the most beautiful high-performance cars you will ever set eyes on. In my search for automotive excellence for this desert road trip it features on the strength of its appearance and its delivery of power. But how does it perform on the road?

Settling into the low-slung driver's seat that swallows you up, in the heart of this formidable machine, you'll feel a keen sense of anticipation, as if waiting for the go-lights on a grid. Needless to say the interior is superb – an exercise in comfort and refinement – but from the moment the displays come alive, your focus will lock onto the road ahead. For this is a driver's car, pure and simple.

The launch is intense, with all the power delivered to the rear wheels. Those first few seconds are marked by adrenaline and joy while your senses fight to catch up with the forces you've just unleashed. And then, like an aircraft levelling after take off, everything begins to settle in. You're travelling at immense speed, and yet the car inspires a sense of tranquillity. This, however, is by no means the equivalent of autopilot.

The One-77 demands commitment at the wheel and it delivers on every level of the driving experience. With a hypercar this peerless, all you need is a seemingly endless stretch of road and an open sky to feel entirely at peace with yourself – which makes the Aston Martin One-77 just perfect for our desert outrun.

ENGINE TYPE	7,312cc V12
NUMBER OF CYLINDERS	12
FUEL TYPE	Premium Unleaded
MAXIMUM OUTPUT	559 kW (760 PS/750 bhp) at 7,500 rpm
MAXIMUM TORQUE	750 Nm (553 lb-ft) at 6,000 rpm
SPRINT TIME TO 62MPH	3.7 seconds
TOP SPEED	220 mph
GEARBOX TYPE	Six-speed automatic transmission

When it comes to assessing excellence in supercars we need to look at the figures. The performance potential is significant, but that's not always a reflection of design and handling. Many top-flight models score highly on all counts and yet there's one other figure that's always worth considering – and that's customer demand. So, with my final choice for this Arabian adventure from Dubai to Bahrain, I'm spotlighting a supercar that unsurprisingly fulfilled all orders before the production run had even begun… the Porsche Carrera GT.

This two-door roadster, produced from 2004 to 2007, quite clearly draws upon Porsche's LMP (Le Mans Prototype) race-car heritage. It's the fastest road-legal car the manufacturer has ever made and the most expensive. It's also come to be regarded as the hardest to tame. Having said that, sometimes the toughest challenges prove to be the most exciting and rewarding.

This is a supercar that's built purely for excellence in performance. Arguably, there are better-looking, sleeker and more menacing supercars on the road, but in my view the Porsche Carrera GT exists to get one job done – and to do so as close to perfection as is humanly possible. In short, it shifts!

Powered by a 5.7-litre V10 engine, producing 605 bhp, you'll need a sensitive foot on the accelerator to take the car from the promised 0–62 mph in 3.5 seconds. It's quite capable of nailing it but such a beautifully lightweight chassis combined with tremendous power can be a handful without care and attention. And this is what sets this GT apart from its rivals. It isn't an easy ride, but once you understand how to harness the capabilities on offer, the car enables a driving experience like no other.

The feathery sensitivity in power delivery is quite incredible and demands skill and precision. It's a little bit like learning to ice skate in that any sense of hesitation slowly evaporates as you recognise just what's possible with confidence and experience. You have a manual six-speed transmission to keep you busy behind the wheel with an impressively lightweight ceramic clutch and a varnished wooden gear knob that is frankly a delight.

ENGINE TYPE	5,733cc V10
NUMBER OF CYLINDERS	10
FUEL TYPE	Premium Unleaded
MAXIMUM OUTPUT	451 kW (613 PS/605 bhp) at 8,000 rpm
MAXIMUM TORQUE	590 Nm (435 lb-ft) at 5,750 rpm
SPRINT TIME TO 62MPH	3.5 seconds
TOP SPEED	205 mph
GEARBOX TYPE	Six-speed manual transmission

Without doubt, in capable hands the Porsche Carrera GT is an almighty machine. It's incredibly fast and simply thrilling to drive. The brakes are reassuringly solid and more than enough to take the sting out of the tail should you find yourself heading too hot into a corner, but you have to think ahead. The car is just so quick that you literally need to be ahead of the game at all times and that is an art in itself. What makes the Carrera GT such a draw is that mastering it is an absolute pleasure.

The interior is boldly functional, built for comfort at speed rather than sheer luxury, and a reminder of the car's racing origins. At full tilt, the Carrera GT feels like an arrowhead. This is where the car's aerodynamic brilliance comes in, with the deep side scoops and rear wing ensuring maximum adhesion to the road. It's one of those supercars that really does make sense when pushed to the maximum.

With the needle in triple figures and the utterly beguiling banshee wail of the engine assaulting your ears, the Porsche Carrera GT feels more like a force of nature than an example of automotive purity. It also features a removable roof, so you can truly appreciate the precision aerodynamics and engineering at work here. It might just be the ultimate combination of driving and racing pedigree, and makes this supercar a fitting final ride as we leave the desert behind and cruise across the causeway into Bahrain.

PORSCHE
CARRERA GT

ROAD TRIP 09

INTO
THE
EAST

INTO THE EAST

• • •

The supercar speaks a universal language. The sight of a high-performance vehicle with wheels turning in anger will always provoke wonder and awe from people all around the world. Of course, it could be said that certain regions focus on particular tastes. The Europeans might celebrate the artistry in combining design and engineering while America makes poetry from sheer muscle power, but what do we find in the east? In answering this question, let's focus on one country that's regarded as a giant in the car manufacturing industry.

Geographically small but economically significant, Japan boasts automotive giants such as Nissan, Toyota, Mazda and Subaru. These are world-beating brands with a well-earned reputation for efficiency, bold design cues and reliability. It's also a country that actively encourages innovation and embraces technology as a vital factor in automotive evolution. What's more, the culture that has fostered a sense of quirkiness as much as formality has given rise to a thriving car modification scene. Throw in the huge popularity at the home of the Formula 1 Grand Prix at Suzuka Circuit and we have an essential stopover on our round-the-world series of supercar road trips.

As we set our sights on the land of the rising sun, it's only fitting that my selection of high-performance vehicles here reflects the values of our host country. I can safely say that my selection will be eclectic, featuring the best supercars from Japan as well as those calling upon characteristics that appeal to its fascinating culture. Above all, I can't wait to cruise the neon-lit streets of Tokyo during a downpour or unleash the throttle on open roads with a view of distant mountains and cherry blossom tumbling in my wake.

SHMEE150'S SELECTION

. . .

LEXUS LFA

NISSAN GT-R NISMO

HONDA NSX

LAMBORGHINI MURCIÉLAGO

NISSAN SKYLINE R34 GT-R

LEXUS
LFA

This is Lexus's first foray into the world of supercars and they've delivered a dream machine! The LFA is a deep-sided two-seater guided by state-of-the-art aerodynamic design. It's impressively chunky but – in keeping with the Japanese spirit – entirely fit for purpose as a road-legal powerhouse of speed, flow and optimum downforce. There's also a vivid sense of muscle here and that extends to the performance it can produce in anger. But before we go anywhere, this is one vehicle that you really need to hear to appreciate.

Under the hood, the Lexus LFA boasts a naturally aspirated 4.8-litre V10 engine. It produces an immense 552 bhp, which is more than enough to spin up the rear wheels from a standstill. Not that you'll hear the sound of flying gravel chips. The roar from this six-speed beast is utterly pulverising. Lean on the throttle and it picks up into a scream that would clear a battlefield. The harmonics and the sound delivery developed by Yamaha are quite incredible as you hit the road and quite unlike anything you've heard from a supercar. Such is the precision in pitch shift that it can even serve as a vital aural cue for timing those semi-automated paddle shifts to perfection. This really is a driving experience that demands full use of both your eyes and ears and that truly makes it special in my view.

The Lexus LFA is a supercar that could only come from Japan. As well as the bold, carbon-fibre composite body shape, making little concession to its European counterparts, Lexus has made full use of technology in both vehicle construction and as an intuitive and deeply satisfying driving aid. Inside, a broad dash features an array of digital readouts and there's a great deal of onscreen activity to serve a car that is as quick and responsive as this one. The car revs so rapidly, for example, that a traditional tachometer needle simply couldn't keep up with it. The display configuration is also completely customisable at the push of a button. Like arranging a home screen on a laptop, this promotes a strong bond between the car and the driver. Ultimately, the LFA feels as if it's been tailor-made.

With a choice of driving modes available, this is an outstanding car primed to deliver the very best performance across a range of conditions. With a top speed of 202 mph, an engine with a whip-fast response and arguably the best sound ever produced by a supercar, the LFA provides a cracking way to kick off my Japanese adventure. Production came to an end in 2012 having manufactured just 500 units, making the Lexus LFA a rare sight on the road, but the sight and the sound of this exclusive high-performance car will be remembered for a long time to come.

ENGINE TYPE	4,800cc V10
NUMBER OF CYLINDERS	10
FUEL TYPE	Premium Unleaded
MAXIMUM OUTPUT	412 kW (560 PS/552 bhp) at 8,700 rpm
MAXIMUM TORQUE	480 Nm (354 lb-ft) at 7,800 rpm
SPRINT TIME TO 62MPH	3.6 seconds
TOP SPEED	202 mph
GEARBOX TYPE	Six-speed automatic transmission

NISSAN
GT-R NISMO

Just the first two parts of this supercar's name should send a chill of excitement down the spine. Anyone with a passion for speed will know that the Nissan GT-R is one of the quickest two-door coupés on the road. Launched in Japan in 2007, ahead of the rest of the world, this thunderbolt on four wheels became a firm favourite in that exclusive club of cars that could take you from 0–62 mph in under 3 seconds. In the light of this rare achievement, Nissan could simply have sat back on their laurels and revelled in the glory. Instead, they built a track-biased supercar with even more punch and power: the GT-R Nismo.

You're still going to get a top speed of 196 mph from the same 3.8-litre Twin-Turbo V6 engine, so what do you get for a car that's significantly pricier than its other family members? Before we get to the performance improvements, it's worth noting that the designers have managed to deliver a supercar that looks even more predatory than the already venomous GT-R. The shape is just that little bit more sinuous and has a bigger spoiler; it looks like they took a hornet and extended its stinger. The Nismo also features different dampers and brake pads, bolstered cooling ducts, a little weight reduction inside the cockpit and a focus on improved downforce and traction. The result? A road-going missile that remains nailed to the tarmac with your foot planted hard on the accelerator.

The engine-shaped heart of this Japanese monster might be the same as the standard GT-R but it beats with more intensity. This time, you'll get an extra 50 PS, taking you just over the 600 mark. Combined with the other refinements, you can feel the difference in the surge of power the Nismo unleashes from a standing start – as well as the overall control you have. The basic GT-R is justifiably recognised as an incredible car, but Nissan have taken things further – simply because they can. As if to prove it, the Nismo posted a 7-minute 8-second lap time at the 12.8-mile Nürburgring Nordschleife circuit, earning it a place as the fourth-fastest production car around the loop since records began.

This is an amazing supercar that demonstrates how the pursuit of automotive excellence can continue to surprise. Just when you think you've found the ultimate drive, another comes along that improves on aerodynamics, power delivery and performance. The Nissan GT-R Nismo shows that the Japanese have earned their rightful place at the top table when it comes to producing some of the most ferocious high-end vehicles in existence today. With their focus on research and development in the field, I have no doubt that a manufacturer like Nissan will continue to push boundaries until the GT-R Nismo's successor arrives. Until then, I thoroughly recommend you jump into 'Godzilla' and celebrate the country's unique flair for delivering an unbeatable drive.

ENGINE TYPE	3,800cc Twin-Turbo V6
NUMBER OF CYLINDERS	6
FUEL TYPE	Premium Unleaded
MAXIMUM OUTPUT	441 kW (600 PS/592 bhp) at 6,800 rpm
MAXIMUM TORQUE	652 Nm (481 lb-ft) at 3,200–5,800 rpm
SPRINT TIME TO 62MPH	2.5 seconds
TOP SPEED	196 mph
GEARBOX TYPE	Six-speed automatic transmission

Any supercar has to stand out from the crowd, but the Honda NSX doesn't just make it on looks alone. It features a jacked-up back end with a subtle lip spoiler, deep windscreen and teardrop-shaped cockpit that wouldn't look out of place on a jet fighter – which is something the designers are said to have called upon for inspiration. The shape may not be to everyone's taste, but if your priority is aerodynamic efficiency, speed, power and handling, then it makes complete sense. Once you pop the hood on the rear-mounted engine bay it becomes completely clear that the engineers refused to compromise on performance delivery.

What you'll find may come as a surprise to anyone who tracked the development of this prized rear-wheel drive, two-seater sports car. The original Honda NSX ran a naturally aspirated V6 with a transverse configuration in which the crankshaft was mounted parallel with the car axles. Midway through development of the new generation, this evolved into a Twin-Turbo V6 with a longitudinal configuration – running front to back. While we might never know how the car would've shaped up with a transverse power plant, we can only congratulate the boffins at Honda, because there's no doubt that the final product is a fearsome machine.

It isn't just the Twin-Turbo that delivers but also three electric motors – with two committed to the front axle alone. Altogether, you're looking at 573 bhp, a phenomenal 645 Nm of torque and a unique power allocation for optimum performance at any time.

As if that wasn't enough, Honda has ramped up the automatic dual-clutch gearbox to nine speeds. On paper alone, this is a hybrid supercar with every intention of chewing up the road in a bid to become one of the most powerful new kids on the block.

Function is very much the focus of the interior but that's fine when performance is the key driver. When I'm focused on pushing a car to the limit, I want information at a glance and that's exactly what the NSX serves up. It's clean, well-thought-through and comprehensive. On jumping in for the first time, one thing you won't fail to notice is a 'quiet' mode that enables the car to draw solely on electric power. On switching to 'sport' and then 'sport plus', you'll experience an incandescent surge in volume and power that shows the sheer range of capabilities the NSX has to offer. Moving through the nine speeds at your disposal is effortless and shows how the additional power from the electric engine can fine-tune the torque to minimise any shortfall in your gear change timing. By the time you switch to 'track', the final driving option, you'll have a clear sense of just how far you can push this car. The additional power to the front wheels – served up just when you need it – boosts confidence as much as torque and grip, but the Honda NSX also handles beautifully. You really will feel like a road-bound jet pilot, as this is as close as you'll come to flying – without wings. It's a sure-fire pick for my Japanese road trip and a supercar that's certain to become a popular draw the world over.

ENGINE TYPE	3,500cc Twin-Turbo V6 + three electric motors
NUMBER OF CYLINDERS	6
FUEL TYPE	Premium Unleaded / Electric Charge
MAXIMUM OUTPUT	427 kW (581 PS/573 bhp)
MAXIMUM TORQUE	645 Nm (476 lb-ft)
SPRINT TIME TO 62MPH	2.9 seconds
TOP SPEED	191 mph
GEARBOX TYPE	Nine-speed automatic transmission

HONDA

NSX

LAMBORGHINI
MURCIÉLAGO

Roaring into our lives in 2001 with production ceasing nine years later, the Lamborghini Murciélago might've made way for the Aventador but it remains a showstopper in every shape and form. If you're looking for a ride that will draw attention while proving to be a thrilling drive, I urge you to consider one of the marque's fiercest and most powerful bulls. Bringing this Italian beast to Japan would be fitting, I think, when placed in contention with the incredible Kawasaki Ninja motorbike. Imagine the precision and poetry in battle between the two-wheel toreador and a car in possession of such brutal, animal power. Watching them dance, weave and lunge would be a truly unforgettable spectacle.

If you asked anyone to sketch a Lamborghini from memory, chances are they'd come up something that compared closest to the Murciélago. In my opinion it's the definitive model when it comes to that familiar wedge – slung low, angular and streamlined to within an inch of its life. It really does embody everything that people adore about Lamborghini and that becomes completely apparent once you're behind the wheel.

At first, the eyeballing you'll come across can be disconcerting. In a sprawling Japanese city like Tokyo or Osaka, you should be prepared for pedestrians to stop and stare. Even in this most formal of cultures, they'll be sure to beam in admiration at the sight of such

a classic European supercar. It's a big vehicle as well, at almost 15 ft long and 6.5 ft wide. Combine that with the deafening noise produced by the 6.2-litre V12 engine and you can forget hoping to go about your business unnoticed. Even jumping in becomes a performance piece as there's no way people can ignore a car with such magnificent scissor doors at full spread.

Inside the car, you'll find a deliciously low ride awaits you. It can feel like a tight squeeze but not in a bad way. This Lambo really does seek to welcome you behind the wheel and make you feel part of the machinery. In urban spaces, that V12 engine growls as you prowl from one block to the next, but out in the Japanese countryside the car's throat opens to produce a howl that could split the sky in two. It honestly sounds like the car is harbouring a secondsond or even a third engine when you're turning the wheel in anger. This is when the shoulder-mounted air intakes come alive and the rear spoiler emerges. Both activate at speed to keep the car aerodynamically primed and at optimum temperature. The deployment is automatic, leaving you to focus on the driving experience.

With an engine capable of producing 572 bhp and a launch control option that can leave you feeling like you're punching through the earth's atmosphere, the Murciélago produces phenomenal speeds in excess of 200 mph. There's more twitch and slide than you might

expect, which may not suit everyone's taste, and with so much power at your disposal the car demands both confidence and respect.

Lamborghini produced several editions that refined the classic model, including a delightful roadster and the outrageous Super Veloce. Each one contributed a little more output but, to my mind, the name Murciélago stands out above all. They don't build cars like the Lamborghini Murciélago any more. Ultimately, it's big, bold and as breathtaking to look at as it is to drive.

ENGINE TYPE	6,200cc V12
NUMBER OF CYLINDERS	12
FUEL TYPE	Premium Unleaded
MAXIMUM OUTPUT	427 kW (580 PS/572 bhp) at 7,500 rpm
MAXIMUM TORQUE	650 Nm (479 lb-ft) at 5,500 rpm
SPRINT TIME TO 62MPH	3.8 seconds
TOP SPEED	206 mph
GEARBOX TYPE	Six-speed manual transmission or six-speed automatic transmission

NISSAN SKYLINE
R34 GT-R

I t's a name that suggests something from the near future. The Skyline GT-R makes me think of a drive that takes you high above the roads of old and into the aerial freeways. It is more conventional than that, but what is perhaps Japan's most celebrated supercar brand always had designs on being ahead of its time.

Nissan introduced the first Skyline in 1957. The first model took the form of a four-door family car but a wide range followed over the years, including an estate version and even a truck. The Skyline quickly earned a reputation for embracing technology in its automotive engineering, which came into its own as Nissan focused on the luxury sports market.

From the late 1960s onwards, the Skyline quickly established a reputation for power and performance

ENGINE TYPE	2,600cc Twin-Turbo Straight-6
NUMBER OF CYLINDERS	6
FUEL TYPE	Premium Unleaded
MAXIMUM OUTPUT	206 kW (280 PS/276 bhp) at 6,800 rpm
MAXIMUM TORQUE	392 Nm (289 lb-ft) at 6,800 rpm
SPRINT TIME TO 62MPH	4.9 seconds
TOP SPEED	155 mph (governed)
GEARBOX TYPE	Six-speed manual transmission

that extended beyond Japanese shores. My favourite has to be the R34 GT-R, released in 1999. A solid, boxy-looking racer with a brash rear spoiler, it lacks the styling of a Porsche 911 Carrera – but moves like no other car!

If you were to judge a supercar by its cornering speed alone, the R34 GT-R would win by a long way. It's a six-speed, four-wheel drive but has a technical set-up that balances the power distribution at any given time. The result is a drive that grips the road like glue on accelerating out of a turn. The traction feels too good to be true, a huge testament to Nissan's engineers, but it makes for a car that will stick to the racing line no matter how you throw it about. The confidence this affords the driver is huge as has been proven with some blistering official track times on the twisting Nürburgring Nordschleife. With a 2.6-litre

Twin-Turbo, straight-six engine delivering 276 bhp, this is a mighty machine that proved hard to beat back in the day.

What's more, time has been kind to the R34, regarded by collectors in the west as a must-have import model. It's a four-seater with a big boot and comes across like a family car with designs on being a prize-fighter. Inside, the dash looks dated but in a delightful way. There are plenty of dials and switches to keep you busy, including a centrally mounted display screen that transports you back in time. The Nissan Skyline R34 GT-R is the final addition to my Japanese road trip. Not only is it a fond homage to this supercar's home country, but it offers a blazing drive while demonstrating that immense automotive power doesn't have to demand a complete workout behind the wheel. In every sense, the R34 hits the mark.

WEST COAST
AMERICA

ROAD TRIP 10

WEST COAST AMERICA

• • •

The open road forms the backbone of this flank of the US. In popular culture, the West Coast of America strikes up images of California sunshine, rolling Pacific breakers and coastal routes custom-made for cruising. Being here is about celebrating the freedom of spirit and adventure as much as feeling the wind in your hair. This is the home of the road trip, as embodied by movies such as *Easy Rider* (USA, 1969), *Thelma & Louise* (USA, 1991), *Vanishing Point* (USA, 1971) and *Duel* (USA, 1971).

When you consider what the region has to offer, it's easy to see why so many are tempted to twist the ignition key and head out on the highway. From the national parks and agricultural valleys, complete with rolling vineyards, to cities such as Los Angeles, San Francisco and San Diego, as well as the heat-baked badlands of the Mojave Desert, there's so much to enjoy by the mile. And with Route 66 and the Pacific Coast Highway on your radar, as well as Sonoma and Sacramento raceways, this is one road trip that's rich in driving history.

It would be tempting to focus on US muscle cars in making my selection, but the fact is that the West Coast is changing. Yes, there's quite probably no better sound than a native, open-throated V8 on the coastal run from Santa Cruz south to Simi Valley, but this neck of America is also way ahead of the pack when it comes to car technology that chimes with the times. As we'll see, California is host to a company that stands at the forefront of developing high-performance vehicles powered by electric engines. And so it's with one eye on fine automobile heritage and another on the future that I present my pick of the finest cars to pursue the American dream… West Coast style.

SHMEE150'S SELECTION

...

TESLA MODEL S P90D

FORD GT

SSC ULTIMATE AERO

MUSTANG ELEANOR

HENNESSEY VENOM GT

TESLA
MODEL S P90D

G one are the days when an electric-powered vehicle conjured only images of milk floats. If any doubters remain, they need look no further than a car manufacturer from California that has torn up the engine rulebook and reinvented the wheel.

Tesla Motors was only incorporated as a company in 2003. With Elon Musk at the helm – who made his name as a co-founder of PayPal and also heads up the reusable rocket transport company SpaceX – this was always going to be a venture that pushed traditional boundaries. Their first production car, the Tesla Roadster, used lithium-ion batteries to power the vehicle for 244 miles on a single charge. With a top speed of 125 mph this was no slouch and rightly generated waves

of excitement among supercar fans. Then came the incarnation that I admire so intensely that it becomes my first choice for this trip.

The Tesla Model S took everything that was promising about the Roadster and turned it into awesome. We're talking about a five-door hatchback with truly breathtaking performance statistics. Consider a car that can boast more than 751 bhp and 966 Nm of torque – exceeding a McLaren 650S – and you'd assume that popping the bonnet would reveal a chunky, gas-guzzling V8 or V12. Not so in the top-spec Model S P90D, powered purely by a rechargeable battery system.

With a new form of power comes a fresh outlook on weight distribution. All the batteries are located at

ENGINE TYPE	Twin electric motors
NUMBER OF CYLINDERS	0
FUEL TYPE	Electric Charge
MAXIMUM OUTPUT	560 kW (762 PS/751 bhp)
MAXIMUM TORQUE	966 Nm (713 lb-ft)
SPRINT TIME TO 62MPH	2.8 seconds ('Ludicrous' mode)
TOP SPEED	155 mph
GEARBOX TYPE	Single-gear automatic transmission

the base of car, allowing boot space at the front and rear. The aerodynamic styling is gorgeous with no need for visual frills when so much innovation is going on underneath. This simple approach flows through to the interior. There, the single biggest hint that this vehicle is at the bleeding edge of technology takes the form of one very large central dashboard screen. It's connected to the internet, enabling the entire car to receive the latest software updates and offers a whole host of driver controls from changing the ride height to the throttle response or opening the sunroof.

When the time comes to start the car things feel decidedly different. There is no engine to fire here. It's a question of waking the vehicle, much like a phone, and then launching with little more than the sound of your heartbeat quickening. The selection of driving modes on offer demand your attention and prove irresistible. If 'Insane' sounds like a riot, Tesla have introduced 'Ludicrous' as a software update on the P90D, reducing 0–62 mph times from an impressive 3.1 to just 2.8 seconds.

With these figures in mind such unconventional mode names are entirely fitting.

Quite simply, the Tesla Model S comes into its own with intense acceleration and grip, yet no screaming motor underneath. Under the rush of air, you can hear the slightest electric tingle from the delivery system but apart from that it's just you and the purest drive on offer today. There's very little roll with such a low centre of gravity and, although it's quite a big vehicle, you'll feel incredibly comfortable behind the wheel.

In terms of juice, the on-board computer highlights charge points on the route you're taking. Then, it's just a question of slotting a plug into the car and heading off for a quick dinner while the battery recharges. It isn't hard to incorporate into your lifestyle and crucially provides epic performance on top of its green credentials. The Model S is even wired with the potential to drive itself, if only laws allowed it, which tells you everything you need to know about Tesla's aspirations as a car manufacturer that's ahead of its time.

FORD
GT

When a supercar sounds this awesome just idling at a standstill, you know you're in for a treat. This is the much-anticipated new Ford GT. It follows on from the now iconic 2005/6 GT models and marks 50 years since the GT40 won the 24 Hours of Le Mans in 1966. That's quite a heritage and behind the wheel of the new model you definitely sense the legacy.

First and foremost, the design is breathtaking. It's a two-seater rear-wheel drive with an all-American heart. Visually, the car is muscular, but it doesn't feel the need to pop its biceps out. The overall aerodynamic engineering offers scoops, slashes, intakes, channels and shapes that come together to create one beautifully contemporary work of automotive art. Even the tail light rings serve a secondsondary purpose as hot air outlets and they look as phenomenal as the dual exhaust horns. Artful use of carbon fibre throughout has created an outstanding power-to-weight ratio for the ultimate in handling. Meanwhile, the active rear spoiler can even serve as an air brake to work alongside the four whopping carbon-ceramic versions that sit behind the 20-in alloy wheels. Inside, the cockpit is both futuristic and minimal with a red starter button in the centre console that screams 'Let's ride!' It's no surprise that the new Ford GT took the prized position of cover model for Microsoft's mighty Forza Motorsport 6 racing video game while still at the design stage.

The Ford GT contains a 3.5-litre V6 EcoBoost Twin-Turbo engine that promises to produce over 600 PS. That's a mighty figure guaranteed to set the pulse racing and together with the seven-speed, double-clutch gearbox this incredible car feels tailor-made for a long, winding coastal run. Along the way, you'll be tempted to pull in at a point overlooking the Pacific breakers, throw open the wing doors and stand back to take a picture of your ride for posterity. It really is one of the most handsome contemporary supercars and one you'll want to share with an appreciative audience. With plenty of beach roads on your journey, perfect for drive-by cruising, the Ford GT is a surefire way to draw the throng from the sand to the sidewalk. It's a supercar set to dazzle, and that's some achievement when contending with the California sun.

ENGINE TYPE	3,500cc Twin-Turbo V6
NUMBER OF CYLINDERS	6
FUEL TYPE	Premium Unleaded
MAXIMUM OUTPUT	>441 kW (>600 PS/>592 bhp)
GEARBOX TYPE	Seven-speed automatic transmission

S S C
ULTIMATE AERO

S peed records are set to be broken. This is why automotive legends endure long after the next fast car comes along. Currently, the Bugatti Veyron Super Sport might wear the crown for the world's fastest production car, although the folks at Hennessey have something to say about that, but in 2007 it belonged to a high-performance vehicle that still sets fire to the tarmac in outright velocity.

SSC North America (formerly Shelby SuperCars Inc), a private, Washington-based sports car manufacturer, launched the SSC Ultimate Aero in 2006. One year later, it rightfully earned a place in history by recording a speed of 256.14 mph. Even now this remains a mighty achievement and not one to ignore when I'm seeking to showcase American supercars on home turf.

Not only is the Ultimate Aero blisteringly quick,

but the car's design makes it an object of beauty. There's a hint of Lamborghini in its menacing shape, with sleek side scoops and low ride height. Even so, the back end is far meatier, which is no surprise when you consider what's ticking inside. We're talking about a 6.3-litre V8, producing an eye-popping 1,287 bhp and 1,508 Nm of torque. But this isn't just a muscle machine. The SSC Ultimate Aero is the Incredible Hulk of the supercar world. It's even claimed that the car could go faster than its world record speed, with an estimated potential of 273 mph. And if you throw in the fact that you have a manual six-speed gearbox to take you beyond the 200 mph mark, I have no doubt you'll be fighting to open up the scissor doors and get behind the wheel.

Inside, you'll find a cockpit that defines automotive minimalism. There's very little going on here beyond the essential dials and switches, and this seems entirely fitting when faced with so much happening on the other side of the windscreen at such high speed. And if you're the kind of driver who immediately seeks out the traction and stability controls and makes sure they're fully deployed, you might want to find another ride; the driver assists you might expect in a contemporary supercar are entirely absent. This is in keeping with SSC's ambitions to create a car that celebrates driver skill as much as performance power.

So, on starting up this savage animal on wheels, you're going to need bags of confidence, a great deal of experience, razor-sharp focus and a clean pair of underpants. As the engine comes alive, you can look forward to 0–62 mph in just 2.8 seconds. You'll also need a lot of empty road, making the Mojave Desert an ideal destination to put the SSC Ultimate Aero through its paces. Just be aware that it'll cover a quarter of mile in just over 8 seconds.

At speed, the blow-off valve kicks in to prevent compressor surge. The result is a high-pitched gobbling sound that accompanies the engine's furious roar, but the SSC Ultimate Aero is far from a turkey. In delivering sheer speed, it doesn't even try to manipulate the engine to sound more pleasing and I consider that to be commendable. It's about naked power, pure and simple. What more do you want?

In short, the SSC Ultimate Aero is a deeply impressive thunderbolt of a supercar and a timely opportunity to celebrate the American automotive industry's constant drive to live the dream on four wheels. Although the Bugatti Veyron Super Sport holds the official production car world speed record, it was no surprise to learn that its main rival – which also features in this road trip – hails from US shores. Meanwhile SSC are hard at work developing a successor to the Ultimate Aero. No doubt when it arrives, records will fall.

ENGINE TYPE	6,345cc Twin-Turbo V8
NUMBER OF CYLINDERS	8
FUEL TYPE	Premium Unleaded
MAXIMUM OUTPUT	960 kW (1,305 PS/1,287 bhp) at 6,075 rpm
MAXIMUM TORQUE	1,508 Nm (1,112 lb-ft) at 6,150 rpm
SPRINT TIME TO 62MPH	2.8 seconds
TOP SPEED	257 mph (verified)
GEARBOX TYPE	Six-speed manual transmission

Cars often play a central role in Hollywood movies and TV shows. From 1968's *The Love Bug* to James Bond's passion for Astons or the Dukes of Hazzard's unmistakable 1969 Dodge Charger, some motors and marques have been defined by their moment in the spotlight. But I have a vehicle in mind for this road trip that made such an impact on the makers of the seminal 1974 car film, *Gone in 60 Seconds*, that it received a star credit in the title sequence. The manufacturer even renamed this Hollywood supercar 'Eleanor' in homage to the film.

What would become an iconic muscle car in movies started life as a Ford Mustang Mach 1 or 'sportsroof'. The two-door sports coupé is unmistakable, even now, with a long front end, short back and a bulging air scoop on top of the bonnet.

The 1971 model, effectively the base for the Eleanor version, was made available to the motoring public in four editions, each with a different power output, but all reliant on the V8 engine and the throaty growl that only a Mustang can make. No doubt the sound proved a big draw to the filmmakers, as did the car's rock star body shape. It's a vehicle made for the mean streets, in my view, which made it ideal to drive in an action thriller about a group of professional car thieves. Even so, in order to meet the stunt requirements on set, the chosen Mach 1 underwent modifications that made it close to indestructible and arguably even more attractive in appearance.

After 250 mechanic-hours in the garage, the Eleanor reappeared with a customised body, roll cage and reinforcements throughout that included chaining down the transmission to keep it place. The seat belt went in favour of a shoulder harness and kill switches were fitted so the stunt driver could shut down the car in the blink of an eye. The classic muscle car had become a brute and its time had arrived to shine on the silver screen.

If you haven't seen the film, I urge you to do so. The stunts are spectacular, including a stunning 128-ft jump and it wouldn't have been the same with any other car. The Mustang Eleanor really is the main attraction and no doubt inspired many movie fans to get behind the wheel of a Mach 1 to pretend it possessed the same character, speed and flair as the *Gone in 60 Seconds* star.

The film was remade in 2000 with Angelina Jolie and Nicholas Cage. This time around, a number of 1967 Mustangs were modified to look like a Shelby GT500, and duly reinvented as the 'Eleanor'. Once again, the car proved to be the star turn, though all but one was wrecked during filming. Such is the vehicle's enduring popularity, the survivor recently sold for a million dollars at auction. Meanwhile, car fans continue to build custom clones of their favourite four-wheeled idol.

So for this journey down the West Coast, I'm sure you'll understand why I'm making a special dispensation to allow a dream supercar to join the ranks. Whether we opt for the original, battle-scarred, Eleanor, the surviving vehicle from the remake or a contemporary copy, this is one legendary high-performance motor that everyone will recognise and cheer along the way.

ENGINE TYPE	6,571cc V8
NUMBER OF CYLINDERS	8
FUEL TYPE	Unleaded
MAXIMUM OUTPUT	>566 kW (>770 PS/>760 bhp)
GEARBOX TYPE	Five-speed manual transmission

MUSTANG
ELEANOR

HENNESSEY
VENOM GT

S ome supercars are incredibly quick but very few are frighteningly fast. On this road trip, the SSC Ultimate Aero is one of the few vehicles that can push the needle deep into 200 mph territory and I'm delighted to include another American-made masterpiece.

Strictly speaking, we should also credit the UK with helping to create the Hennessey Venom GT. It's a supercar based on the Lotus Exige and assembled on British shores under the guidance of John Hennessey and his Texas-based tuning house, Hennessey Performance Engineering. This might sound like an unusual genesis for any car. When I tell you that the Venom GT is quicker than a Bugatti Veyron (albeit unofficially), such a creation becomes more like a work of genius.

So, what do we have? A Lotus tub for sure, but it's barely recognisable when side-by-side with the Exige. Such are the mighty scoops that have been extracted from the sides that the Venom GT looks skeletal by comparison. Bold shaping, moulding and aerodynamic refinements have been introduced across the car, which is longer and, weighing in at a featherlight 2,743 lb, also leaner than the donor vehicle. There's no doubt this record-breaking supercar bears little resemblance to the Lotus (a peerless performer in its own right) and that's before we've even lifted the engine-bay cover.

ENGINE TYPE	7,000cc Twin-Turbo V8
NUMBER OF CYLINDERS	8
FUEL TYPE	Premium Unleaded
MAXIMUM OUTPUT	928 kW (1,261 PS/1,244 bhp) at 6,600 rpm
MAXIMUM TORQUE	1,566 Nm (1,155 lb-ft) at 4,400 rpm
SPRINT TIME TO 62MPH	2.7 seconds
TOP SPEED	270.49 mph (verified)
GEARBOX TYPE	Six-speed manual transmission

It's a monster, pure and simple. That Hennessey have succeeded in fitting a 7.0-litre Twin-Turbo V8 into the back while maintaining optimum balance is a miracle. The gold lining inside the engine cover is perhaps a fitting frame for this work of automotive art. It simply throbs with power – even before the ignition is engaged. And when it does come alive, you'll take a step back in sheer awe. The noise is deep and intense, like a muscle car ready for a rampage, which can only turn your thoughts to throwing open the door and jumping in.

Inside the Venom GT, the control layout is focused so you don't have to search around the dash looking for the info you need. Everything is tightly arranged behind the wheel and it works beautifully. You'll also find a six-speed manual gearshift, an empowering sight for any driver preparing to fire up this astonishingly quick car.

Like the SSC Ultimate Aero, this is a superhero machine that requires an extended strip of tarmac if you're going to make it soar. Fortunately, the West Coast of America is the perfect region. With flat, scrubby desert landscapes to the south promising razor-straight roads and mountainous backdrops, this is the ideal stage to take the car to an incendiary top speed of 270.49 mph. That's an insane figure and can only be truly appreciated by experiencing it for yourself on what has to be the road trip of a lifetime.

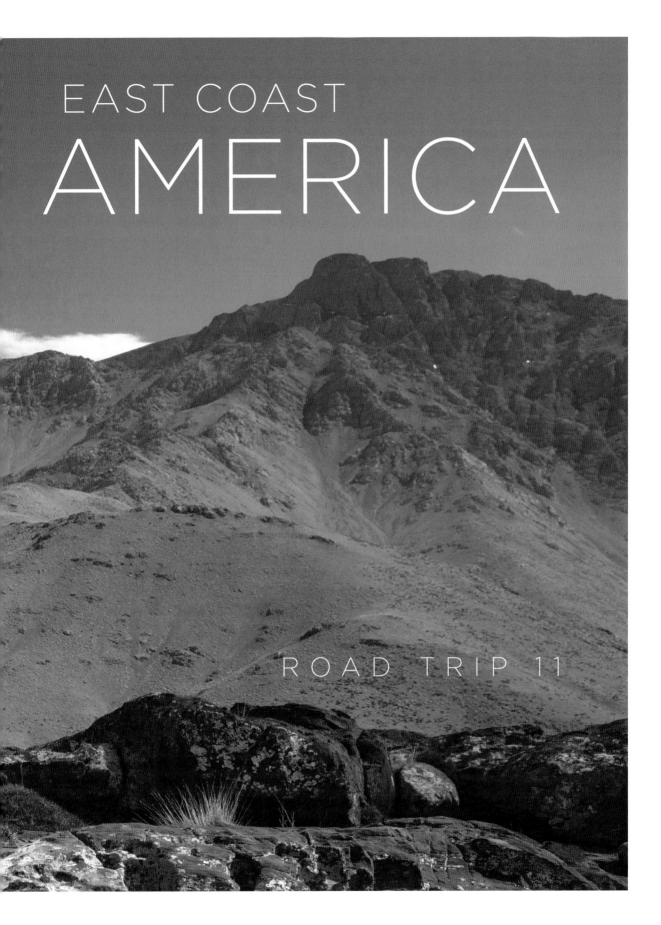

EAST COAST
AMERICA

ROAD TRIP 11

EAST COAST AMERICA

• • •

We swap sides for this next run and I'm not talking about trading the driver's seat with the passenger. We're simply jumping from the West Coast to the eastern flank, which promises a very different but equally rewarding road trip.

This is still very much an opportunity for open-road cruising. America is a huge country, after all, with long routes between cities on both sides. But while the West Coast may revel in its laid-back vibe, the east is often said to be more fast-paced. With a denser population, different climate and varied terrain, we're looking for supercars that offer both pace and space as well as comfort and luxury driving.

From the forested roads of Maine and Massachusetts in the north down to Florida's Alligator Alley and everything in between, the Eastern Seaboard offers a huge range of driving experiences. It's also host to world-class cities such as Boston, New York, Washington D.C. and Miami, which offer plenty of scope for urban cruising, as well as providing famous backdrops for those essential supercar photo opportunities.

With US Route 1 running for 2,300 miles from Fort Kent in the north to Key West in the south, this is a road trip that promises adventure at every turn.

SHMEE150'S SELECTION

...

RANGE ROVER
AUTOBIOGRAPHY

FERRARI TESTAROSSA

ROLLS-ROYCE WRAITH

BENTLEY CONTINENTAL GT V8 S

CADILLAC CTS-V

R A N G E R O V E R
AUTOBIOGRAPHY

British carmaker Land Rover has long held a world-class reputation for making luxury, four-wheel-drive utility vehicles. They're instantly recognisable, calling upon values of trust, performance across all terrains, raw strength and prestige. What's more, these are high-end vehicles that aren't afraid to be seen with dirty mud flaps. The manufacturer's Range Rover flagship range is a case in point, producing SUVs designed for hard work and play, which makes it a fitting start point for my selection.

It's fair to say that the Range Rover Autobiography will get you to your destination, whether you stick to East Coast roads or choose to go cross-country through forest or swampland. This is a supreme all-terrain 4x4 that can

handle anything you throw at it. We might be looking at a hefty two-tonne beast and the most expensive edition on the market, but you do get more bang for your buck. Under the bonnet (at the top of the range) you'll find a 5.0-litre Supercharged V8 engine capable of producing a mighty 625 Nm of torque. That'll give you 0–62 mph in just over 5 seconds, a top speed of 140 mph and no sense of hesitation when it comes to driving through floods, reed beds or roads blocked by rock falls. It is a supreme workhorse that inspires confidence and that's just the start of it.

As well as delivering standout power and performance, Range Rover's Autobiography edition provides a five-star driving experience. You settle into leather seats, each of

ENGINE TYPE	5,000cc Supercharged V8
NUMBER OF CYLINDERS	8
FUEL TYPE	Premium Unleaded
MAXIMUM OUTPUT	375 kW (510 PS/503 bhp) at 6,000 rpm
MAXIMUM TORQUE	625 Nm (461 lb-ft) at 2,500–5,500 rpm
SPRINT TIME TO 62MPH	5.1 seconds
TOP SPEED	140 mph
GEARBOX TYPE	Eight-speed automatic transmission

which is capable of providing a programmable massage. And while this 4x4 is busy working on your shoulder knots you can fire up the on-board surround camera system to keep an eye on all your blind spots. This is no gimmick. In a vehicle that's quite capable of taking on woodland gullies as well as parking in tight spots, it's a vital navigational aid. Likewise, the electronic air suspension system is fitted with manual override, adding to the sense of being in complete control. Everything is within easy reach and with all the lumps and bumps removed from the ride (as well as your lumbar region), you won't be struggling to hit the right switch.

I genuinely adore this edition, and not just for the driving experience. It's unmistakably a Range Rover

but the bodywork refinements sets the Autobiography apart from its predecessors. From the 22-in, seven-spoke alloy wheels to the adaptive Xenon headlamps as well as double-glazed windows, you'll feel like a secondsret service agent, whether you're driving through a metropolis or tearing up backwoods lanes.

Even if you're simply at the wheel to enjoy the journey, there's a whole host of features to ensure that the vehicle does the dirty work for you, such as a simple but really wonderful function (for when your hands are full) that allows you to open the boot by swiping your foot under the rear bumper. Even before you jump into the driving seat, this is an all-terrain supercar that's got your back in every conceivable way.

It's been a while since we featured a Ferrari in a road trip and only fitting that we fire one up on our East Coast adventure. Introduced in the mid-80s, in the form of the 512TR and F512M, the Testarossa is a two-door coupé delivering power to the rear wheels. In many ways, the back quarter is the bit to watch with this car. Not only is that where you'll find Ferrari's masterpiece 4.9-litre flat-12 engine, it's also famously wider than the front end. Not by a huge margin, but enough to keep you on top of your game behind the wheel. Because, combined with the weight, you're looking at stepping out at speed and you want to be sure that every time this delivers thrills not spills.

In a strange way, I think this makes the Testarossa one of the most well-balanced cars Ferrari has built. Yes, there is a steep learning curve with this one that demands a cautious climb, but once you're up there it provides a driving experience that revels in the concept of being on the edge. And on a road trip that promises many miles of winding forested roads, I know this is a feature that many will find irresistible. It's also worth noting that the Ferrari Testarossa was the go-to car of choice for *Miami Vice*'s cool detective, Sonny Crockett. The TV show immortalised the car and its appearance is sure to be appreciated should you finish your road trip cruising the strip behind South Beach.

You won't find a rear spoiler on the Testarossa. With the mid-mounted engine providing such a sweet centre of gravity, cooled by massive go-faster side vents, the handling is defined by just how far you're prepared to take it. This is a great way to measure driver ability, I think, while inspiring a level of healthy respect for a high-performance car that you don't always feel behind the wheel of contemporary models. Technology has made life easier when your foot's on the accelerator, but these cars are powerful beasts that, ideally, should never be taken lightly. The Testarossa strips away the safety net and places the responsibility squarely in your lap.

If coming to terms with the car's drivability is a challenge, you'll find it's a joy once you've mastered it. The engine delivers 490 Nm of torque, the capacity to rocket from 0–62 mph in 5.3 seconds and to hit a top speed of 180 mph. Modern-day supercars might be able to go faster but simply nothing compares to an old-school ride this noisy and thrilling. It's a mid-80s' poster car that really does deserve a soundtrack from the era with unashamed guitar solos to accompany every corner that you'll be sure to fishtail around. I consider it to be a guilty pleasure, in many ways, and I have no doubt that on this trip down the Eastern Seaboard you'll love it just as passionately as I do.

ENGINE TYPE	4,943cc Flat-12
NUMBER OF CYLINDERS	12
FUEL TYPE	Premium Unleaded
MAXIMUM OUTPUT	291 kW (396 PS/390 bhp) at 6,300 rpm
MAXIMUM TORQUE	490 Nm (361 lb-ft) at 4,500 rpm
SPRINT TIME TO 62MPH	5.3 seconds
TOP SPEED	180 mph
GEARBOX TYPE	Five-speed manual transmission

FERRARI
TESTAROSSA

When all you have to do is press a button to close the rearward-hinged coach door, you know you're inside a roller. This one has been designed from top to toe for maximum comfort, style and prestige, but you'll also find a sporting sensibility alongside the sense of effortless decorum that we've come to expect from the manufacturer. Ladies and gentlemen, I present... the Wraith.

The 2013 edition isn't the first Wraith to float out of the Goodwood-based UK manufacturer. Rolls-Royce released their first edition in 1938 and it fast became the last word in high-end motoring. Some might say releasing a contemporary version was a risky move. Having taken one for a spin, I can safely say the gamble paid off. It's simply incredible, not just to look at and

drive but to relax inside and watch the East Coast of America pass by at speed.

Essentially, it's a powerful four-door coupé that calls upon the chassis of Rolls-Royce's hugely popular Ghost. Then again, describing it as a coupé is a little bit like categorising Windsor Castle as a detached house. As an exercise in luxury driving, it's just head and shoulders above all competitors. The leather seats are butter-soft which reassures as you settle in to admire the interior. The indulgence extends to the dashboard, where the central control screen is hidden behind a wooden panel that lifts back on launch. It's a minor detail, but this is the level Rolls-Royce operate on in serving up their seriously superior car. And if you're still in doubt, look up! The starlight headliner is made up of 1,340

ENGINE TYPE	6,592cc Twin-Turbo V12
NUMBER OF CYLINDERS	12
FUEL TYPE	Premium Unleaded
MAXIMUM OUTPUT	465 kW (632 PS/624 bhp) at 5,600 rpm
MAXIMUM TORQUE	800 Nm (590 lb-ft) at 1,500–5,000 rpm
SPRINT TIME TO 62MPH	4.6 seconds
TOP SPEED	155 mph (governed)
GEARBOX TYPE	Eight-speed automatic transmission

ROLLS-ROYCE
WRAITH

individual lights to create an incredible constellation effect that mirrors the stars in the sky on the night the first ever Phantom came off the production line in 2003. It's a grand but refined touch, serving to make you feel a part of the Rolls-Royce family and is entirely in line with a high-performance luxury car that reaches for the skies in so many ways.

So, what's it like on the road? Can a manufacturer with a focus on cosseting the driver and passengers roll up its sleeves to deliver a car with a knockout punch? It certainly looks powerful, like a Ghost pulled back on its haunches. Starting up the engine gives us a good idea of what's in store. The noise of the Wraith is strikingly understated at first but this is entirely in keeping with the Rolls-Royce vibe. When you put your foot down and feel

your chest compressing, you expect the engine to begin howling. Instead, it simply delivers without making a big song and dance, just what you'd expect from this mobile member of your house staff. It's an incredible experience as it quickly brings you up to speed without fuss.

The Wraith is no lightweight machine, but put your foot down and it's ferocious as it leaps into action. Under the long, stately bonnet sits a V12 Twin-Turbo capable of producing 624 bhp and 800 Nm of torque, which makes it the most powerful Rolls-Royce ever made. This is a huge achievement for a car that's so staggeringly quiet and relaxing to drive, making this road trip one to share with friends. So, give the chauffeur the week off and prepare to enjoy what Rolls-Royce promise to be 'a debonair gentleman's GT'.

BENTLEY
CONTINENTAL GT V8 S

This is a big car in so many ways. Size is clearly everything when it comes to the Bentley Continental GT V8 S, from the ample interior space to the thumping great muscle engine and the smile on your face when you realise just how much you can cane it. But big isn't the only touchstone to describe this luxury cruiser on wheels. Along with its power, it's also incredibly smooth.

The Continental GT V8 S is an updated version of a popular model first released in 2003, though Bentley have used the Continental name on vehicles since the 1950s. From the start, Bentley's aim was to produce a high-performance motor that wasn't just comfortable and classy but sporting and – crucially – reasonably affordable. Bentley succeeded on all counts, earning a reputation for producing a muscular but prestigious grand tourer that packed a serious punch. Since then, the Continental GT name has emblazoned several incarnations – from a convertible to a Le Mans edition – but my firm favourite has to be the GT V8 S. The muscle engine isn't new but the outputs have been refined and improved to make what I consider to be the finest edition yet.

So, with added grunt the 4.0-litre Twin-Turbo beast under the bonnet can now produce 520 bhp, take you from 0–62 mph in 4.5 seconds and – with the hammer down – reach a speed of 192 mph. It's an attractive prospect, but additional refinements to the way this car handles are what make the experience stand out. An uprated chassis, lowered suspension, revised stability control, rear-lip spoiler and custom fender vents help

ENGINE TYPE	3,993cc Twin-Turbo V8
NUMBER OF CYLINDERS	8
FUEL TYPE	Premium Unleaded
MAXIMUM OUTPUT	388 kW (528 PS/520 bhp) at 6,000 rpm
MAXIMUM TORQUE	680 Nm (502 lb-ft) at 1,700 rpm
SPRINT TIME TO 62MPH	4.5 seconds
TOP SPEED	192 mph
GEARBOX TYPE	Eight-speed automatic transmission

to keep the car incredibly settled. Even on the kind of gritty roads you might find after a rainstorm in South Carolina, the Continental leaves you feeling like you're driving over a bed of silk. Yes, it's heavy, but strong torque and acceleration when you need it turns that to your advantage. It's also surprisingly agile, which is where this grand tourer shows its sporting ambitions.

Ultimately, the Bentley Continental GT V8 S is a luxurious coupé that calls upon banks of power and delivers them peacefully and smoothly – a rare find. As a result, you can look forward to a road trip that doesn't feel like a challenge but rather a pleasure cruise, and this

will appeal if you're bringing friends or family along for the ride. The leather seats accommodate four very comfortably with masses of luggage space in the boot and a wood, carbon-fibre or aluminium veneer finish to the interior that feels classy to the fingertips. You'll also find an 8-in central touchscreen console with state-of-the-art satnav capabilities and an awesome in-car sound system. Sometimes, it isn't about how white your knuckles can turn as you fight with the steering wheel but rather the pleasure of simply travelling in comfort, confidence and style. The Bentley Continental GT V8 S offers this in spades without any compromise to performance.

L et's return to an American-born motor for the last pick for our road trip. This is in no way a token gesture. The mighty V8-powered super-saloon I have in mind has rightfully earned its place in the East Coast pack.

As a brand, Cadillac is to cars what Coke is to soft drinks. It's known the world over and very much a product of the American Dream. People love the look of a Caddy and the lifestyle it suggests and, with the CTS-V, that's one driven by style, muscle and the capacity to delight and thrill in equal measure.

What we have here is effectively an athletic edition of the Cadillac CTS – the go-to car for executives across the USA since 2002. The CTS looked great, provided a

comfortable interior and delivered a rock-solid drive. The CTS-V ticks all these boxes but boasts a massively improved engine and a sense of aggression. With serious aerodynamic and performance refinements to back it up, this new incarnation presents itself with its tie pulled loose, top button undone and the departmental meeting furthest from its mind. Quite simply, the new Cadillac CTS-V is all about fast and furious fun behind the wheel.

The addition of a letter 'V' on the end of the car's name might not seem like much, but it represents a monster engine. Under the bonnet, enlarged to accommodate the air intakes, Cadillac has implemented a 6.2-litre supercharged V8. That it's derived from the engine built for the Corvette Z06 just hints at this road-

CTS-V

ENGINE TYPE	6,162cc Supercharged V8
NUMBER OF CYLINDERS	8
FUEL TYPE	Premium Unleaded
MAXIMUM OUTPUT	478 kW (650 PS/640 bhp) at 6,400 rpm
MAXIMUM TORQUE	854 Nm (630 lb-ft) at 3,600 rpm
SPRINT TIME TO 62MPH	3.8 seconds
TOP SPEED	200 mph
GEARBOX TYPE	Eight-speed automatic transmission

legal car's racing aspirations and the power is harnessed beautifully. Even though you're looking at a fearsome 640 bhp, 854 Nm of torque and a top speed of 200 mph, added the sense of control at speed is striking. With an eight-speed transmission on hand everything comes together in a perfect storm of performance power. That the CTS-V has gone head-to-head with the likes of the BMW M5 and Mercedes-Benz E63 AMG is a testament to the skill and engineering invested in this rear-wheel drive dream. Along with the mighty engine set-up, you'll find state-of-the-art suspension and dampers that provide precision control and instil a sense of confidence as you seek to bring out the best in the car.

I also want to credit Cadillac for their finishing touches with this car. While the performance potential is unquestionably impressive, I love how the running light strips have been incorporated into the headlights. This gives the car a low, wide stance after dark. In fact, anyone driving ahead might look in their rear-view mirror and be forgiven for thinking the vehicle behind is scowling menacingly. The five-seat edition is just perfect to pack in a posse for this East Coast adventure, while Cadillac have furnished the interior to be sure you'll travel in comfort and style. From the neat splash screen that travels across the dash display on ignition to the manufacturer's much-admired Cadillac Cue entertainment system, the CTS-V is packed with tech and driver assists to provide you with a tailor-made road experience that's as swift as it is satisfying.

ROAD TRIP 12

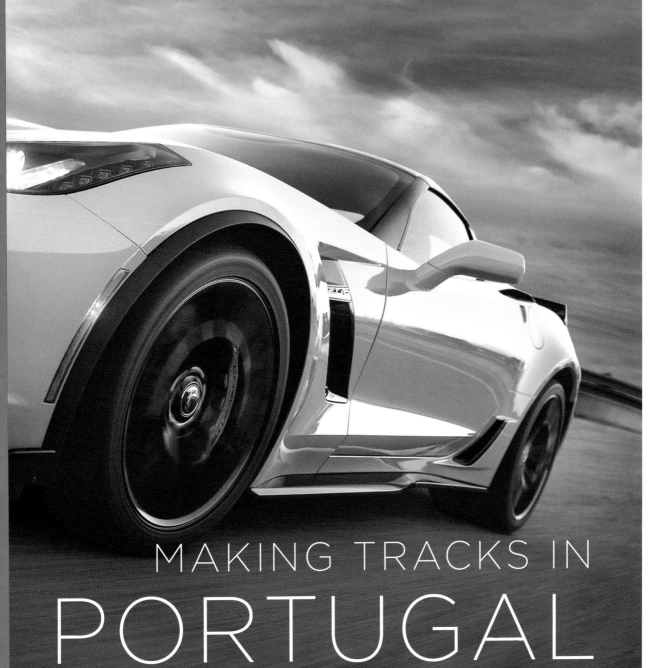

MAKING TRACKS IN
PORTUGAL

McLAREN
P1

For those who wish to ease into this track day gently, look away now. What I have to introduce you to here is a hypercar that's capable of mind-bending performance. Before you've even completed a circuit, whether as a passenger with a professional driver or behind the wheel with your eyes on stalks, the McLaren P1 will have redefined speed at every turn.

The car is considered to be the follow-up to the peerless McLaren F1 and combines hybrid power with a level of technological sophistication found in a Formula 1 car. As we all know, McLaren have form in the latter and have led the way for decades in developing automotive engineering. So, it's fair to say that on paper the P1 promises to be deeply impressive.

On track, it goes way beyond all expectation, as you might expect with a car boasting a race mode that is illegal to use on public roads. One touch of a button lowers the hydraulic suspension by 2.1 in – bringing the wheels up into the arches. It also tilts the rear wing – to

ENGINE TYPE	3,799cc Twin-Turbo V8 + KERS unit
NUMBER OF CYLINDERS	8
FUEL TYPE	Premium Unleaded / Electric Charge
MAXIMUM OUTPUT	673 kW (916 PS/903 bhp)
MAXIMUM TORQUE	980 Nm (723 lb-ft)
SPRINT TIME TO 62MPH	2.8 seconds
TOP SPEED	220 mph (governed)
GEARBOX TYPE	Seven-speed automatic transmission

29 degrees – producing a mighty 600 kg of downforce at 160 mph. With your foot on the accelerator, the transformation prevents this savagely fast performance car from lifting off.

Even before you've taken the first corner sequence at Portimao – a triple-turn layout that requires perfect timing to hit the apex each time – it's clear that the P1's power is absolutely phenomenal. Powered by a Twin-Turbo V8 working alongside a custom electric motor, the combined output is a storming 903 bhp and 980 Nm of torque. That's enough to pin you to the seat and demand that your brain works in triple time to keep up. As if to hammer home the level of performance power on offer, each time the turbo spools down it does so with a whiplash crack. By the time you've cleared the fifth turn and are seeking to catch your breath on the straight, that crack urges you onwards – into a new dimension of driving.

The McLaren P1 is a masterpiece of the modern automotive age. With the capacity to go from 0–62 mph in 2.8 seconds, and a (limited) top speed of 220 mph, it's like a 650S on steroids but with outstanding energy efficiency.

There are quicker cars, but in terms of precision handling the P1 takes to the circuit with ballerina-like grace, and in a race situation that can give you the winning edge. The body is toned, sculpted and scooped to the bone and serves as an object of beauty as much as a track weapon.

Inside the cockpit, the transparent hood panels connect you to your surroundings. With the scenery flying by in a blur, it really does feel like a road-hugging rollercoaster ride. This is thrilling stuff that overloads your senses and is so deeply responsive at every turn that within a couple of laps you'll feel confident enough to start pushing at what is already an absolute powerhouse of a contemporary supercar. McLaren have always had a flair for balance and handling and that's served up here at every turn. If you're track-side, watching someone else at work behind the wheel, there's plenty to admire. Such is the temperature of the air from the exhaust that the McLaren P1 quite literally spits fire while hugging any line like a slot racer. I am deeply impressed and excited by this hypercar, and it's a fitting way to kick off a track day nobody will forget.

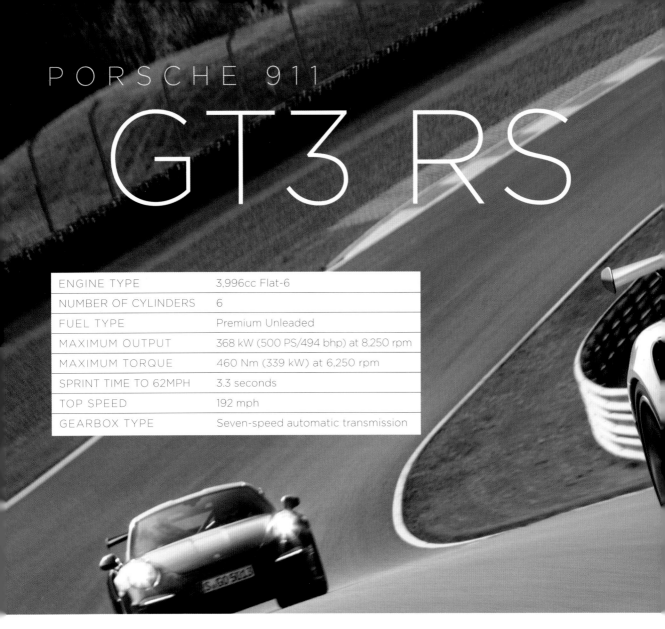

PORSCHE 911
GT3 RS

ENGINE TYPE	3,996cc Flat-6
NUMBER OF CYLINDERS	6
FUEL TYPE	Premium Unleaded
MAXIMUM OUTPUT	368 kW (500 PS/494 bhp) at 8,250 rpm
MAXIMUM TORQUE	460 Nm (339 kW) at 6,250 rpm
SPRINT TIME TO 62MPH	3.3 seconds
TOP SPEED	192 mph
GEARBOX TYPE	Seven-speed automatic transmission

E veryone knows and loves the 911. Since the late 60s this rear-wheel-drive, two-door sports car has become commonplace on our roads. Each edition has brought new performance capabilities while retaining that familiar and much-loved body shape with its curved roof shell.

The 911 GT3 RS doesn't step out of line in this respect. The GT3 edition itself has been around since 1999. It came into existence as a high-performance version of the 911 and quickly established itself as a successful track car. It's lightning-quick and incredibly responsive, thanks to a fully-adjustable suspension set-up and massive braking capabilities.

This brings us to the GT3 RS, which is positively venomous. The rear wing sets the car apart from its predecessors. It isn't the first but it's huge and a measure of just how much downforce this car demands to stop it from becoming airborne. The GT3 RS uses lightweight components throughout the car and a unique magnesium roof to full effect, making it less heavy; it looks both leaner and meaner than the standard model.

As well as efficiencies in aerodynamics and weight, Porsche's engineers have extracted 494 bhp from the 4.0-litre flat-6 engine, and equipped the driver with maximum control through a seven-speed paddle-shift sequential gearbox. This is where the car really

begins to do the talking, because out on track it's a powerhouse. When you brake hard into a corner, the car properly sits down, digs in and gets the job done, while on straights it punches hard thanks to 460 Nm of torque. With a top speed of 192 mph, the only thing that stands between you and a record lap time is your ability at the wheel.

Fortunately, the GT3 RS is set up to help you bring out the best in the car. The bucket seats are firm but accommodating and provide a crystal-clear sightline. There are no rear seats, just a roll cage, while on closing the door the handle strap serves as a nice reminder that weight-saving informs every feature of this car. It all adds to the sense of excitement when you fire up the engine and feel the chassis hum with anticipation.

Out on circuit, the GT3 RS sets the track ablaze. Granted, you have to work pretty hard, but the car does its best to reward you. As a driver – or a racer – you're right there in the moment every secondsond of the way. Thanks to a firm ride, seamlessly quick gear-shifts and pitch-perfect power delivery, this rampantly race-happy 911 provides an absolutely thrilling experience and the chance to go top when it comes to setting the fastest lap times with your mates.

Many supercars sit back on their rear haunches, as if preparing to strike. Then there's the Chevrolet Corvette Z06, which looks so compressed at the back end that you feel like it might actually leap. It has a huge, long front end, swollen in places to accommodate the monstrous 6.2-litre V8 engine and it features magnificently handsome body styling from end to end – this car is sure to win any track day on appearance alone.

But the Corvette Z06 doesn't just look the business. Unleashed, with 641 bhp and a similar torque number, it's blisteringly quick. The car – a version of the venerated Corvette Stingray – makes its presence known when the sound from that mighty engine resounds around the racetrack. Spectators who have headed out to Portimao's fast tenth turn will hear the sound of thunder on the home straight and know just what's coming. It's an incredible war cry, delivered through four exhaust pipes and a chastening sound for other drivers. Yes, it can be deafening behind the wheel but I like it when the exhaust valve is open and singing its heart out.

Inside the Z06, strapped in nice and tight, you're presented with a fine-looking digital display that's completely configurable depending on your choice of drive. From 'wet weather' mode to 'eco' and 'race', you can transform the set-up and also the display to foreground the most critical info. It presents you with a different experience with every turn of the dial.

What Chevrolet has set out to do here is create a track-ready car that appeals both to a driver with basic race smarts as well as a pro. In the manual transmission model, for example, the car mimics the heel-and-toe technique that only the very best racers can pull off – effectively blipping the engine while braking with the same foot to ensure the revs stay high on the downshift. It's incredibly difficult to pull off and learning how to do it demands close tuition from someone who knows what they're doing to avoid a one-way trip into the gravel trap. So, it's a weight off my mind when the Z06 achieves it seamlessly as I drop a gear, as well as a delight to hear.

The active rev matching is just the kind of race feature that makes the car so enjoyable at speed. There's seemingly boundless power on offer, taking you from 0–62 mph in 3.2 seconds, and promising a top speed of 185 mph and if you're the kind of driver that likes to feel the car snap before it gets into shape then this is the seat-of-the-pants performance vehicle for you.

Another cool feature is the opportunity to plug an SD memory card into the dash and record your lap via the on-board cameras. With the option to overlay the footage with performance readouts, you can use the technology to refine your racing technique or simply impress your friends. In short, the Corvette Z06 is a mighty racer that combines fun with flat-out fury and for a track day you can't ask for anything more.

ENGINE TYPE	6,162cc Supercharged V8
NUMBER OF CYLINDERS	8
FUEL TYPE	Premium Unleaded
MAXIMUM OUTPUT	478 kW (650 PS/641 bhp) at 6,400 rpm
MAXIMUM TORQUE	881 Nm (650 lb-ft) at 3,600 rpm
SPRINT TIME TO 62MPH	3.2 seconds
TOP SPEED	185 mph
GEARBOX TYPE	Seven-speed manual transmission or eight-speed paddle shift transmission

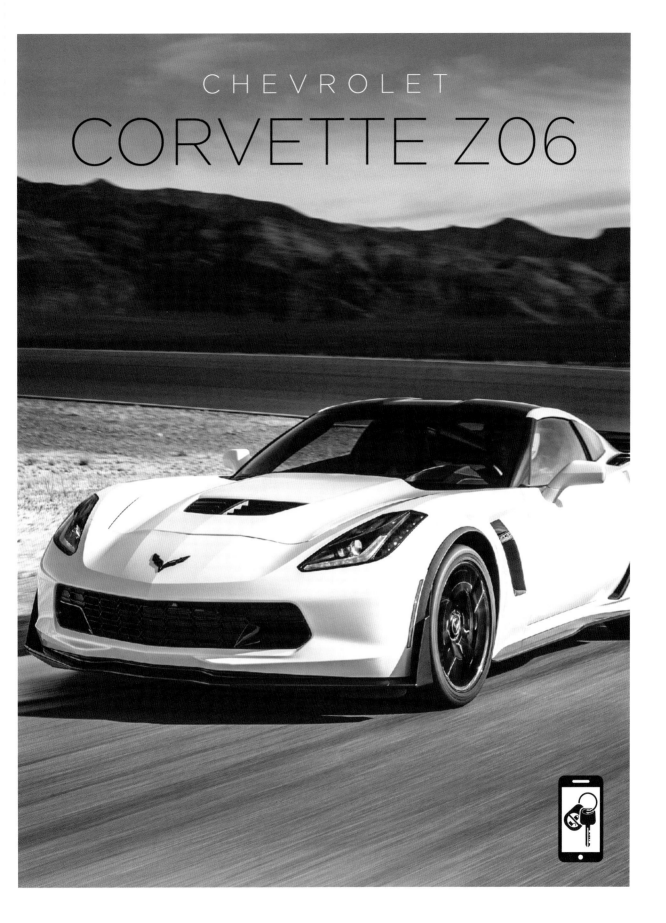

I could have nominated the Ferrari F12berlinetta for this track day. This 2012 rear-wheel-drive grand tourer quickly made a name for itself on the grounds of intense power and traction, which makes it ideal for punishing the Portimao Circuit. But taking the F12 would be remiss when you consider the racing refinements that have gone into the F12tdf. The result is a supercar that's just a little bit quicker, angrier and hungrier for the chequered flag.

This is a limited edition, with Ferrari producing exactly 799 units. One look at this rare beast and you'll be completely unsurprised to learn that every single car has been snapped up. It is absolutely beautiful and I love the slashed side vents made so iconic by the 250 GTO. As well as being able to draw comparisons with the FF and the 458, I feel that both the F12berlinetta and the new F12tdf (the initials come from its inspiration, the Tour de France) are directly descended from Ferrari's classic 1960s' race car. You have the same long, sweeping bonnet and compact back end, with aerodynamic styling that borders on the poetic, but the F12tdf takes things to another level in terms of sheer anger.

Along with significant weight savings in the chassis and bodywork and cosmetic changes front and back, the F12tdf's 6.3-litre V12 engine has been upgraded to produce 769 bhp. Out on track, this now takes you from 0–62 mph in 2.9 seconds and has an intense top speed of more than 211 mph.

The interior chimes with Ferrari's focus on driving purity. You'll feel strangely calm on settling in and placing your hands on the wheel. Nothing is out of place. Everything is just so. When you reach for the ignition you'll wonder if the car runs on a mixture of snake venom and furious hornets. The noise is just insane and bodes well as you take the F12tdf for a speculative lap around the circuit.

The power is unquestionable. It's a Ferrari, after all. Mindful of unruly but still outstandingly fun stable-mates like the Testarossa, the key is in how this prancing horse handles. After just a couple of corners including elevation changes for good measure, it's safe to say the F12tdf performs to perfection. The combination of balance, power, traction, suspension and grip enables you to sweep through turn after turn without compromise. It's a pure apex-runner with rock-solid and responsive brakes on entry and harmonious acceleration and transmission shift that turn your exits into a powerhouse run. The F12tdf might be a limited edition model – and elsewhere the F12berlinetta is certainly no coaster – but for a memorable track experience with leading lap times you need this tour de force from Maranello.

ENGINE TYPE	6,262cc V12
NUMBER OF CYLINDERS	12
FUEL TYPE	Premium Unleaded
MAXIMUM OUTPUT	574 kW (780 PS/769 bhp) at 8,500 rpm
MAXIMUM TORQUE	705 Nm (520 lb-ft) at 6,250 rpm
SPRINT TIME TO 62MPH	2.9 seconds
TOP SPEED	>211 mph
GEARBOX TYPE	Seven-speed automatic transmission

FERRARI

F12tdf

FRANCE
AND FURIOUS

PAGANI
ZONDA R

As if the Zonda wasn't powerful enough, Pagani have gone further with this ultra-limited edition run. There are just 15 Zonda R's in existence and they stand out for being custom-made for the track.

Before we get to the standout performance statistics, it's important to appreciate the car's incredible form. The design is just breathtaking; the car looks more like a missile than a motor. It's also quite beautiful and simply flows from front to back with aerodynamic perfection. At the back, a huge vent provides a glimpse of just what is propelling this car and it promises a truly special experience. Some high-performance cars struggle to contain their engines but not this one. It's strikingly tidy, as if effortlessly assembled and yet another reason why the Zonda R is such a compelling prospect to drive.

Then there's the weight – or lack of it. Pagani have gone out all-out with carbon fibre here to produce a machine that clocks in at a remarkable 1,070 kg. This featherlight construction is key to the Zonda R's ferocity. In other hands, with a 6.0-litre V12 engine fitted in the back, it might simply be a design destined to perform a backflip. Instead, Pagani have created a hypercar that not only sticks to the track on race slicks but also sets the circuit on fire.

ENGINE TYPE	5,987cc V12
NUMBER OF CYLINDERS	12
FUEL TYPE	Premium Unleaded
MAXIMUM OUTPUT	552 kW (750 PS/740 bhp) at 7,500 rpm
MAXIMUM TORQUE	710 Nm (524 lb-ft) at 5,700 rpm
SPRINT TIME TO 62MPH	2.7 seconds
TOP SPEED	>217 mph
GEARBOX TYPE	Six-speed manual transmission

What we have here is an engine that can produce 740 bhp and 710 Nm of torque. Off the line, you can expect 0–62 mph in 2.7 seconds and a top speed on the straight of more than 217 mph. At full throttle it feels like a dream, while braking and doesn't turn it into a slippery nightmare. The slowdown is intense but uniform and you'll soon be going beyond the brake boards knowing you can still hit the apex of each corner. It's this combination of crazy speed and assured handling that sets the car apart from its rivals. If further proof is needed, a Zonda R is on record for completing a lap of the Nürburgring in just 6 minutes 47 seconds.

For all the fury this track-only hypercar creates, there's also a great deal of sound. The Zonda R is deafeningly loud and nowhere is that more apparent than inside the cockpit. Pagani's commitment to speed means that sound insulation has been left behind and your ears could be ringing for some time after you've left the track. There's a very good chance that you'll feel that it just isn't possible to go any quicker. It won't stop you trying because this Italian track car wants to deliver, and in the right hands it'll produce results that are impossible to beat. Unless, of course, you have a chance to jump into the Zonda Revolución – an updated and improved version of the Zonda R that pushes performance car evolution into even more extreme territory. For Pagani, the pursuit of perfection is a driving force.

FERRARI

FXX K

Here's another prototype car that deserves a moment under the spotlight. The Ferrari FXX K is based on the Ferrari LaFerrari, upgraded to take over the track. It hasn't been built for competition but simply for the pursuit of performance perfection. What this means is that the car has been designed and assembled with no regard for rules and regulations but only an insatiable appetite for sheer speed. It's a laboratory experiment that in time may well come to benefit road-legal Ferraris, making a drive in one the chance to sample a taste of things to come. In view of the impeccable Maranello marque and the noble intention behind the car's existence, it easily makes the cut in my selection.

The back-end design provides the first clue that Ferrari are doing things differently. While the LaFerrari sports an active rear wing that retracts to little more than a lip, the focal point of the FXX K has to be the bold side wings that come to frame the tail of the car. They're unconventional to say the least, but given Ferrari's reputation they also make the drive ahead a thrilling prospect.

The K in the name relates to KERS (Kinetic Energy Recovery System), which hints at the level of technology Ferrari have applied. Drawing upon the system for harvesting energy under braking that's been refined by Formula 1, the FXX K features a naturally aspirated V12 tuned to produce 837 bhp. Combine this with the hybrid power and the sum total is 1,021 bhp – alongside 900 Nm of torque – simply astounding.

A seven-speed, dual-clutch transmission helps to reach a top speed of 220 mph, making Paul Ricard one of a select few tracks capable of letting drivers truly wring this car's neck. It's a formidable, hardcore beast, with aerodynamic advances producing 50 per cent more downforce than the Ferrari LaFerrari. This kind of setup doesn't just inspire confidence on a high-speed circuit but also does so in challenging conditions. With so much grip accompanying the velocity, the FXX K is equally capable of claiming records in the wet as much as the dry.

Inside, you won't find the comfort features of the Ferrari LaFerrari, but that's in keeping with the uncompromising commitment to speed. The seat is fixed within the carbon tub with all the controls and telemetry data aligned to assist you in pushing the FXX K to the limit. It's comfortable, for sure, but your attention will be on the track in this ride rather than searching for the radio dial. If you're going to reach for anything as you're hurtling around the circuit, in fact, it'll be one of four performance settings: 'qualify', 'long run', 'manual boost' and 'fast charge'. Each one modifies the driving experience to ensure you extract the very best from the car at any moment in time around the lap. It's a thrilling experience and an absolute joy to include in the line-up for this track day where speed is of the essence.

ENGINE TYPE	6,262cc V12 + HY-KERS unit
NUMBER OF CYLINDERS	12
FUEL TYPE	Premium Unleaded / Electric Charge
MAXIMUM OUTPUT	761 kW (1,035 PS/1,021 bhp)
MAXIMUM TORQUE	>900 Nm (>664 lb-ft)
SPRINT TIME TO 62MPH	<3.0 seconds
TOP SPEED	220 mph
GEARBOX TYPE	Seven-speed automatic transmission

ASTON MARTIN
VULCAN

This is a limited edition run from a manufacturer who knows how to make peerlessly quick cars. The Aston Martin Vulcan calls upon both the DB9 and Vantage as inspiration but this won't be gracing public roads. What we have here is a mighty track conqueror that looks as good as it performs.

The most exciting thing about this car for me is the engine. Aston Martin have taken their 7.0-litre V12 engine and turned a mighty powerhouse into something utterly immense. Wielding 789 bhp, this

hypercar is so mighty that the lucky owners of the 24 in the production run will receive an extensive track-training programme.

As well as boasting incredible performance potential, with top speeds far in excess of 200 mph, this has to be one of the most beautiful designs you'll ever see on the circuit. Often, prototype cars employ so many carefully crafted aerodynamic parts that function eclipses form. With the Vulcan, you're presented with a sumptuously sleek beast. In particular, the long bonnet and exquisite cockpit shell look both organic and imperious. The rear

ENGINE TYPE	7,000cc V12
NUMBER OF CYLINDERS	12
FUEL TYPE	Premium Unleaded
MAXIMUM OUTPUT	>588 kW (>800 PS/>789 bhp)
GEARBOX TYPE	Six-speed automatic transmission

wing is significant, but it doesn't overwhelm and while the lines are futuristic they never lose sight of the car's heritage. Then there are the rear lights, which reinvent the concept by taking the form of a blade cluster. The result is both dramatic and innovative and completely sums up the car. Ultimately, the Vulcan is way ahead of the game, and bodes well for the shape of future road cars to come from the Aston marque.

On the track, this incredible prototype car handles with the finesse and grace of the Aston One-77. The added power and bite brings things to a whole new level, of course, and with the rear-wheel drive you'll quickly come to appreciate the training programme thrown in with the car. The car is positively venomous, spitting flames from the side-exhaust as you rocket around the circuit, but there's also balance, as incredible braking capacity and traction keep you on the racing line. In a way, it's a shame that this amazing car is such a rarity, but that's not why I'm selecting it for our track day. The Aston Martin joins the pack on the strength of its awesome power and sheer beauty, both at speed and in the paddock – where you're sure to draw a crowd of admirers.

McLAREN
P1 GTR

For good reason, we selected the McLaren P1 for our track day at Portugal's Autódromo Internacional do Algarve in Portimão. There, I wanted to showcase McLaren's awesome harnessing of modern technology to create a high-performance hybrid supercar that could take the road by storm. The mechanical might on offer with the P1 is simply astonishing, making the prospect of an even more ferocious McLaren something we can't ignore. Under consideration here, on a circuit where the focus is on raw speed and race chops, is a special model built by the British manufacturer for track use only.

A limited edition and lightning-fast car, the P1 GTR was first announced to mark the 20th anniversary of the McLaren F1 GTR's victory in the 1995 24 Hours of Le Mans. This version is 50 kg lighter than the production car and has an altogether more aggressive stance. The fixed rear wing is even primed for DRS, which is an exciting development. This is the 'drag reduction system' that has become a familiar feature in Formula 1, in which an adjustable flap opens up to improve straight-line speed and closes on braking to restore downforce for cornering.

To propel you on the way, you can call upon a formidable 986 bhp from the 3.8-litre Twin-Turbo hybrid V8. With race suspension, a fixed ride height, a brand new exhaust and slick tyres, you're looking at a car with a massive hunger for lap records.

The P1 GTR's sheer power should not be underestimated. With this in mind, McLaren have provided an intensive training programme for buyers of the 35 units produced. From an induction session to seat configuration and helmet design, along with time in the simulator ahead of a test day, this is a car that demands respect as much as quick reflexes. The level of engineering and aerodynamic excellence here means you'll need to be at the very top of your game to really push this car so it rides the ragged edge. That makes an opportunity to strap into the cockpit, pull down the door and take it around the circuit such a thrill. The P1 GTR gives you so much scope to push the boundaries of your race craft and even reach your pinnacle as a driver. Without doubt, in good hands it'll turn a track day into an exhilarating demonstration of performance excellence.

ENGINE TYPE	3,799cc Twin-Turbo V8 + KERS unit
NUMBER OF CYLINDERS	8
FUEL TYPE	Premium Unleaded / Electric Charge
MAXIMUM OUTPUT	736 kW (1,000 PS/986 bhp)
GEARBOX TYPE	Seven-speed automatic transmission

LAMBORGHINI
SESTO
ELEMENTO

A low ride height brings several benefits to any high-performance vehicle. It reduces the centre of gravity, improving handling at speed, and it looks awesome. There's nothing more aggressive than a supercar so close to the ground that it's practically part of the tarmac, and you won't get much closer than the Lamborghini Sesto Elemento. The gap is incredibly tight between chassis and track, perhaps a reflection of the uncompromising approach this prototype car takes in pursuit of circuit domination.

Appearance-wise, you're looking at a Lamborghini that could be completely made from super-lightweight carbon fibre with a deliciously dark matte finish. That's just how pure it appears in terms of material and from where the Sesto Elemento (Italian for 'sixth element', represented by carbon in the periodic table) derives its name. What's so clever here is that the body design appears uncharacteristically organic for a marque so renowned for incorporating clever geometric shapes. Step back, however, and that familiar Lamborghini signature becomes apparent in subtle but vital streamlining across the car's hood, edging and flanks. It's both sophisticated and intimidating and I love it.

You'll find further engineering aerodynamic innovation in the hexagonal air ducts that stripe the mid-engine hood. This further adds to the car's formidable appearance, and just hints at the power it contains. The 5.2-litre V10 can generate 562 bhp and 540 Nm of torque. This will take you from lights out on the grid to 62 mph in a Bugatti Veyron-baiting 2.5 seconds, followed by a top speed of 200 mph. On the scales, the Sesto Elemento comes in at just 999 kg, creating an incredible power-to-weight ratio and the prospect of improving your personal bests on the circuit.

You won't find much inside the cockpit, fittingly for a super-light track car. Even the dashboard is pretty much absent but rendered impressively in true Latino style. Strapped into what must be the most minimal foam seat on the market, your focus is on the button-rich race wheel, the six-speed transmission with paddle shifts and the belief that simply focusing on where you want this car to be on the track at any moment in time will take you there.

It's set up to be one of those instinctive drives in which you feel like a component of the car rather than a rider struggling to stay in the saddle. The low ride height works wonders here. It might not be much use on suburban streets, but on a smooth track surface you can simply floor the car and experience how it feels to be pinned back by the full force unleashed.

With power delivered to all four wheels, this laser-sharp Lamborghini builds on the marque's reputation for mechanical grip and pinpoint-precision handling at high speed and this is where you'll gain an advantage over so much of the competition. Yes, it's formidably fast, but the car can switch and turn without going wildly out of shape. That builds confidence in you as a driver and shavings from each lap time. Not only will that bring the Sesto Elemento into contention at the top, it could make it unbeatable.

As you will in all the cars selected for this track day, you'll feel truly special behind the wheel of Lamborghini's highly successful experiment in aerodynamic efficiency and engineering power. As for the circuit, I hope you'll agree it's the perfect stage for the kind of high-speed laps that only a select few have experienced on four wheels.

ENGINE TYPE	5,204cc V10
NUMBER OF CYLINDERS	10
FUEL TYPE	Premium Unleaded
MAXIMUM OUTPUT	419 kW (570 PS/562 bhp) at 8,000 rpm
MAXIMUM TORQUE	540 Nm (400 lb-ft) at 6,500 rpm
SPRINT TIME TO 62MPH	2.5 seconds
TOP SPEED	200 mph
GEARBOX TYPE	Six-speed automatic transmission

BEST OF
BRITISH

ROAD TRIP 14

BEST OF
BRITISH

• • •

For our final road trip, I want to return to my home country. This is where I first fell in love with supercars and where learned to bring out the best in them. Great Britain may not be the biggest country we have visited on our world tour but it offers varied and spectacular driving landscapes that offer a huge range of thrills and challenges.

In particular, I intend to focus on the more rugged regions, from the Welsh hills and valleys to Scotland's mighty vistas and out to the Isle of Man. With its annual TT motorbike race, its roads seem purpose-built to pit man against machine at speed. It instils a sense of healthy respect, with magnificent ribbons of tarmac that demand the utmost concentration.

While guaranteeing a great time, what I can't promise is good weather. We're unlikely to enjoy the dry heat of Dubai or crystal skies of the Alpine peaks. Instead, there'll be a very good chance of anything from mist and drizzle to outbreaks of rain and even sleet or snow if we head out in the winter months. We can hope for sunny spells – and often the British weather delights – but it is unpredictable. But this makes a car adventure even more joyful. Essentially, you have to be prepared for anything and not just from the skies. I've lost count of the number of times I've taken to a rural pass thinking I have the road

to myself only to find myself crawling behind sheep as a farmer leads his flock out to pasture. But this isn't a complaint. It's all part of the package. In fact, you won't find anywhere in the world like this when it comes to road trips and that's a precious thing. Whether you're heading out alone or with a group of friends, all you can say for sure is that there's bound to be a surprise in store and an entertaining story to share when you return home.

For this final road trip, I plan to pick an eclectic mix of cars. These aren't vehicles that are celebrated for one stand-out feature. They perform well on every count and represent the best of British. I'm also keen to reflect those halcyon days when motoring first empowered the ordinary man and woman to explore the country by road. That said, there are no vintage open tops here demanding a crank handle to start the engine, but I will find you modern-day incarnations to reflect that heritage.

Every car on offer gives you the potential for having fun. This is something often overlooked when the focus is on power, performance, torque and aerodynamics. These are all essential elements and give us reasons to admire a work of automotive art but a good car should also be a joy to drive – even when the weather or farming livestock conspires against you.

SHMEE150'S SELECTION

· · · ·

LOTUS EVORA 400

CATERHAM 620S

MORGAN AERO 8

ZENOS E10 S

ARIEL ATOM 500

MORGAN 3 WHEELER

The original Evora was met by much excitement when unveiled in 2009. Why? Because this was a brand new road car from Lotus, the first in nearly 15 years and as a manufacturer of future classics, they have form. From the Elite to the Elan and the Elise, this is a British marque with an impressive flair for design and engineering.

Powered by a 3.5-litre V6, the two-plus-two seater Evora went down a storm on British shores and beyond, but I'm leaving the Evora behind for my road trip around the country. Why? Because Lotus went on to release the Evora 400. But the latest version doesn't just feature the old model with a body tuck and engine tweak. With so many components replaced, it's effectively a different car under the same name…

On the exterior, you're still looking at the familiar, impressive shaping that made the Evora so popular. The shark-like profile and long back – to accommodate those rear seats – is still present but, while it's a little leaner and meaner than the original, there's nothing in the car's appearance to reflect the weight reduction undertaken here. In reality, Lotus examined every component to find a way of making it lighter. As a result, the Evora 400 has shed over 40 kg from its original design, which primes it beautifully for the new engine set-up.

While Lotus has opted to power the car with the same V6 engine, it no longer produces 276 bhp. Thanks to such a comprehensive overhaul and supercharger, this astounding supercar now boasts 400 bhp. That's very close to doubling the output, and deserves our admiration. You'll certainly give thanks as the car takes you from 0–62 mph in just 4.2 seconds. With the capacity to deliver a top speed of 186 mph, there's no doubt that the Lotus Evora 400 packs a punch, but how does it fare on hillside roads flanked by dry stone walls? Even with an impressive powertrain to call upon, you need to know that the car has the handling smarts to see you through without scraping the paintwork or worse.

The good news is that the Evora 400 isn't just quicker than its predecessor. With stiffer springs, a lower ride height and beefier brakes working alongside the improved power/weight ratio, it's effectively a celebration of mechanical grip. You really can point, turn or burn rubber in this car without wincing or hoping for the best, and that instils confidence as much as sheer enjoyment.

On the inside, you'll find that Lotus have revised the dash to make it far more accessible than the original, with a snappier transmission that feels more in tune with your needs as a driver. It's loud but not lairy and delivers a drive that feels equally at home on the motorway as it does on the high road. For a trip into the outlying reaches of the UK, where supreme handling is essential in both wet and dry conditions, this is my go-to British sports car.

ENGINE TYPE	3,456cc Supercharged V6
NUMBER OF CYLINDERS	6
FUEL TYPE	Premium Unleaded
MAXIMUM OUTPUT	298 kW (406 PS/400 bhp) at 7,000 rpm
MAXIMUM TORQUE	410 Nm (302 lb-ft) at 3,500 rpm
SPRINT TIME TO 62MPH	4.2 seconds
TOP SPEED	186 mph
GEARBOX TYPE	Six-speed manual transmission or Six-speed automatic transmission

LOTUS

EVORA 400

CATERHAM
620S

T he Caterham Seven has been in existence since 1973. It's a low-cost, stripped-back, lightweight and high-speed little gem that famously took over from Colin Chapman's Lotus Seven design. They're road-legal but so track-happy that an entire race series is dedicated to these impressive rear-wheelers. In addition, the Caterham Seven is renowned for being available to customers in kit form as well as the finished article. As a result, this is an affordable supercar that appeals to both the driver and the garagista in equal measure.

Caterham has evolved the Seven blueprint over the

years to produce a number of excellent editions. The 620S is tailored for road use, with its airflow-optimised nose cone and race-developed cooling package and has always been one my favourites. But I'm equally fond of this reduced weight range for the way the cars behave on the track. They sit beautifully, with bags of torque and power and present a driving experience that's as stripped back and thrilling as the car itself.

In particular, I'm drawn to the 620S. With a 2.0-litre Ford Duratec engine under the front bonnet, it's capable of producing 310 bhp and 297 Nm of torque. And with a 0–60 mph time of just 3.4 seconds, this dazzling

ENGINE TYPE	1,999cc Supercharged V4
NUMBER OF CYLINDERS	4
FUEL TYPE	Premium Unleaded
MAXIMUM OUTPUT	231 kW (314 PS/310 bhp) at 7,700 rpm
MAXIMUM TORQUE	297 Nm (219 lb-ft) at 7,350 rpm
SPRINT TIME TO 62MPH	3.5 seconds
TOP SPEED	145 mph
GEARBOX TYPE	Five-speed manual transmission

creation is quick enough off the mark to compare with the likes of the Porsche 911 GT3.

It's an assault on the senses at speed, with the din of the engine and an oncoming hurricane blast in the cockpit to contend with, but the chances are that on a summer's evening you'll even catch some midges in your teeth with your wide smile behind the wheel. Yet again, Caterham have created a car that guarantees an adrenaline rush delivered on purity of performance and so it has to take a stage of this road trip to make the journey truly memorable.

The Caterham 620S wears its British origins with pride. The long bonnet and open-top, two-seater cockpit don't just echo the Lotus Seven heritage but also remind me of another old-school reinvention we're set to spotlight for this road trip: the Morgan Aero 8. The two models are worlds apart but both prove exceptionally well-suited for tearing up country lanes with enough ferocity to send the crows flapping from the treetops. What Caterham have created here is a car that threads and slides through turns just beautifully. Whether you're rotating around a track, seeking out a fast lap time or are intent on enjoying the sense of freedom that comes with propelling a sports car through the best roads the UK has to offer, the 620S is both sure-footed and seriously quick.

MORGAN

This is a return to the Aero line for a manufacturer with a cut-glass reputation for creating simply gorgeous roadsters. Seeing the convertible, with the long bonnet and those stately, sweeping side arches, the prospect of beetling through country lanes one summer afternoon is irresistible. Should the weather conspire against you, a snap-on hardtop is available. At once this transforms the car into the perfect ride for gliding up country house drives at dusk with the headlamp beams leading the way. Whatever your preference, the Morgan Aero 8 is a quintessentially British sports car and has to be a prime contender for this road trip.

Underneath the iconic bonnet sits a 4.8-litre V8, which immediately tells you that this car is no slouch. It can produce 362 bhp and a hugely impressive 490 Nm of torque, with the potential for 0–62 mph in just 4.5 seconds. If you've opted to drive with the roof down it really is a question of hanging onto your top hat. And with a choice of six-speed manual or automatic transmission, Morgan have tailored the Aero 8 to help you hit the road in whatever way makes you feel comfortable. With a low centre of gravity, you can expect the kind of handling finesse that will make light work of dodging ditches and coping with country roads where the camber might

ENGINE TYPE	4,799cc V8
NUMBER OF CYLINDERS	8
FUEL TYPE	Premium Unleaded
MAXIMUM OUTPUT	270 kW (372 PS/362 bhp) at 6,300 rpm
MAXIMUM TORQUE	490 Nm (361 lb-ft) at 3,400 rpm
SPRINT TIME TO 62MPH	4.5 seconds
TOP SPEED	170 mph
GEARBOX TYPE	Six-speed manual transmission or
	Six-speed automatic transmission

catch others off-guard. It is, in many ways, both fun and furious, and that's a combination you don't hear often!

For all the nods to tradition, this is also a sports car that doesn't overlook technological and design innovation. The rear-opening clamshell boot is a lovely touch and serves as an introduction to the way that the new Aero 8 has embraced an original but suitably restrained modern-day design sensibility. Jumping in behind the wheel, the interior feels refreshed and updated but still retains that Morgan charm. As a compact and cosy two-seater, this is a roadster that's almost purpose-built for you and a companion to make the most of the open road. Morgan plans a limited production run and, in keeping with a car that really does bring out your personality, you can have it finished in any colour combination you choose.

Ultimately, there's something irresistible about taking on British country roads in a convertible with the top down. It helps you to engage with the landscape as much as the roar and burble of the engine. The Morgan Aero 8 provides plenty of V8 volume as you barrel along at a deeply impressive pace, but there's still enough scope to chat with your passenger and turn a mundane journey into a rip-roaring adventure.

There are no doors on this car. Quite literally, you have to jump in – and there's no cooler way of getting behind the wheel than that.

What we have here comes from another British manufacturer with impressive automotive chops that have earned it a premium place in the market for lightweight track-day sports vehicles. Norfolk-based Zenos – co-founded by former Caterham boss, Ansar Ali – claim that the E10 series is the most exciting thing to come out of the region since Boudica, and they might just be right. If such a statement brings a smile to your face, setting your eyes on the E10 S is sure to leave you grinning because it looks like lots of fun.

Structurally, the car combines a unique aluminium backbone with a carbon-composite cockpit. There's no roof to set off the absence of doors, while the focus is very clearly locked upon the driving experience. You have a 250 bhp, 2.0-litre naturally aspirated Ford mid-mounted engine. With 400 Nm of torque, this is capable of covering 0–62 mph in 4 seconds and can take you to a top speed of 145 mph. Crucially for a track-day car, however, the Zenos E10 S combines its exhilarating power potential with incredibly nimble handling. It's also road-legal, which opens up the possibility for extracting maximum enjoyment.

You'll feel surprisingly comfortable on buckling the seat harness, grasping the wheel and preparing to put the vehicle through its paces. Some might expect something so track-focused to compromise, but not here. By contrast, the display system is straight to the point, shorn of frills and there are no driving assists on offer. The absence of traction control and ABS might leave you feeling wary, but that's fine. It gives you an opportunity to get to grips with the car and ease into a full appreciation of just how beautifully it connects with the road. It makes for a more rewarding sense of confidence, while the whizzing sound of the wastegates opening on throttle lift-off proves quickly addictive.

This is no crazy horse, but it packs a punch all the same and you'll enjoy the ride no end. With a five-speed transmission at your disposal (plus an option to go to six) you'll soon appreciate just how close the E10 S gets to that rare combination of excitement, fun and driving purity.

ENGINE TYPE	1,999cc Turbocharged V4
NUMBER OF CYLINDERS	4
FUEL TYPE	Premium Unleaded
MAXIMUM OUTPUT	186 kW (254 PS/250 bhp) at 7,000 rpm
MAXIMUM TORQUE	400 Nm (295 lb-ft) at 2,500 rpm
SPRINT TIME TO 62MPH	4.0 seconds
TOP SPEED	145 mph
GEARBOX TYPE	Five-speed manual transmission

ZENOS
E10 S

ARIEL
ATOM 500

If we assembled a supercar leaderboard combining speed with pure fun, there is only one name that would sit at the top. It looks like an open-wheeler racing car but it's road-legal. It's also far smaller than performance kings like the BMW M5 and Porsche 911 and yet it's quite capable of giving machines of that calibre a run for their money – even leaving them in the dust. We're talking about the Ariel Atom and I can assure you that it's an absolute blast to drive.

For this road trip, however, my focus is on a limited edition that's even more of a thrill-seeker than the original. On paper, when you consider the power-to-weight ratio, the Ariel Atom 500 sounds crazy. In reality, it's exactly that, in the most thrilling way you can imagine.

We should begin with the chassis, because the British-manufactured Atom effectively wears one on the outside and to devastating effect. The two-seater cockpit is located deep within these sleek gold tubes, overlooked by a significant air scoop. With an F1-style nose, fully adjustable, double-wishbone suspension tuned by Lotus, carbon-fibre bodywork and an enormous rear wing, there's no doubt that this car draws heavily on the track for inspiration. But this is no pretend performance racer. It's the real deal.

For a car weighing just 550 kg, the engine spec is astounding. The 3.0-litre V8 produces a colossal 500 bhp, which should make this machine undriveable. But it doesn't. Such is the level of engineering and aerodynamic harmony – with suspension sprung to perfection – the Ariel Atom 500 will take you from 0–62 mph in just 2.3 seconds.

With a low centre of gravity and a racing seat that immediately makes you feel a part of the car, taking the Ariel Atom 500 up to speed feels entirely within your control. It might snap and squirm as you put the hammer down and leave you feeling like a mighty wave is set to break over your head, but the mechanical grip is just so good that all four wheels stay planted. Here's where the fun-factor kicks in and with an extra seat for a passenger, it's an experience to be shared.

If you have the chance to take the Ariel Atom 500 or any earlier model onto the track, then I urge you to do so. But while it's sure to delight on unrestricted straights and chicanes, it's equally rewarding just pootling along on public roads. With the wind in your face and the roar of the engine, the open cockpit serves to intensify the performance factor, while the six-speed transmission with paddle shifts can't fail to keep you focused. You'll also find this limited edition features a comprehensive LCD display. It provides info on all the car's vital signs at a glance, from speed to engine temperature and even includes the chance to record telemetry.

The Ariel Atom 500 delivers an unbeatable driving workout that isn't rocket science to master. Yes, you'll need some racing skills to extract the very best from this car, but even while you're getting up to speed, it'll delight with every lightning-quick upshift.

ENGINE TYPE	3,000cc V8
NUMBER OF CYLINDERS	8
FUEL TYPE	Premium Unleaded
MAXIMUM OUTPUT	373 kW (507 PS/500 bhp) at 10,600 rpm
MAXIMUM TORQUE	385 Nm (284 lb-ft) at 7,750 rpm
SPRINT TIME TO 62MPH	2.3 seconds
TOP SPEED	168 mph
GEARBOX TYPE	Six-speed automatic transmission

ENGINE TYPE	1,983cc S&S V-twin
NUMBER OF CYLINDERS	2
FUEL TYPE	Premium Unleaded
MAXIMUM OUTPUT	61 kW (83 PS/82 bhp) at 5,250 rpm
MAXIMUM TORQUE	140 Nm (103 lb-ft) at 3,250 rpm
SPRINT TIME TO 62MPH	6.0 seconds
TOP SPEED	115 mph
GEARBOX TYPE	Five-speed manual transmission

To finish our journey – not just through the outlying regions of the UK, but the world tour we've undertaken to celebrate the speed, power, performance and flair of the supercar – I'd like to introduce you to a personal favourite. It's unlike any vehicle I've selected so far, and as soon as you lay your eyes on it you'll appreciate why.

I adore the Morgan 3 Wheeler so intensely that it featured in my personal collection. It was only right that my car, with a custom blue wrap to match my McLaren 12C Shmeemobile, became known as the Shmee Wheeler.

British-based and family-owned, the Morgan Motor Company has been producing legendary, hand-built sports cars since 1909. On the surface, very little has changed in terms of the unique and hugely respected design, and why should it when Morgan has created such timeless classics? The 2011 edition of the company's iconic Three Wheeler is a case in point. It presents itself as a vintage motorcycle melded with the ball turret of a B17 bomber. With two wheels at the front and one at the back, a tubular spaceframe chassis, barrel-shaped hull and an exterior mounted 82 bhp V-Twin engine, it spells serious fun. On top of all that, the car is seriously nippy,

MORGAN
3 WHEELER

achieving 0–62 mph in 6.0 seconds, and a top speed of 115 mph. It also handles beautifully, with a low centre of gravity and those sturdy front wheels maintaining great balance and stability.

What can be distracting is the response from the people you pass. Quite simply, it's impossible to zip by unnoticed in this delightful motor, and you'll feel duty-bound to wave and jab the thumbs-up at everyone. This really is an invitation to smile on wheels, just one small component of the fun to be had here. With a Mazda five-speed gearbox to help you on your way, you'll feel both connected to the road and a sense of British heritage. After a few miles out in the country, you'll be wondering why cars evolved at all from the wonderful Edwardian era of motoring that this car celebrates. It's a joy to drive, with a great deal of modern performance value on offer and won't just brighten up your day. Some vehicles are purely functional; others are built to get you places rapidly or with design in mind. The Morgan 3 Wheeler offers everything rolled into one while delivering a drive that leaves you feeling that it's good to be alive in this day and age. For living the dream, you can't get much better than that.

Thank you for sharing in my dream road trips around the globe – I hope you've enjoyed the ride. Now you have experienced my favourite supercars and the roads they were designed to drive on, I thought it only fair to share with you my top 14. It's been a very difficult task to choose just one amazing car from each trip to place in an imaginary supercar garage. Each of the cars in this collection has its own individual defining element that makes each one stand out from the rest in their own special way, but after much careful consideration, here is my Shmeemobile wishlist. My true dream garage...

McLAREN F1

SHMEE150 DREAM GARAGE

MERCEDES-MAYBACH S600

KOENIGSEGG ONE:1

PORSCHE CAYMAN GT4

FERRARI F40

MERCEDES-BENZ 300 SL GULLWING

KOENIGSEGG REGERA

ASTON MARTIN ONE-77

LEXUS LFA

FORD GT

ROLLS-ROYCE WRAITH

McLAREN 675LT

PAGANI ZONDA R

MORGAN 3 WHEELER

PHOTOGRAPHER CREDITS:

ROAD TRIP 01 – LONDON CALLING
Main photo © Sam Moores Photography
Aston Martin DBS © Lucian Bickerton
McLaren F1 © Willem Verstraten Photography
Rolls-Royce Phantom © Man Of Yorkshire
BMW i8 © Bas Fransen Car Photography
McLaren 650S Spider © Photocutout
Jaguar XJ220 © Jaguar MENA

ROAD TRIP 02 – DESTINATION EUROPE
Main photo © Bentley Motors Limited shot by James Lipman
Ferrari FF © Sebastian T Photography
Bentley Bentayga © Bentley Motors Limited shot
by James Lipman
Mercedes-Maybach 600 © Daimler AG
Aston Martin Rapide S © Ben of Streetcars London
Audi RS 6 © ABT Sportsline GmbH

ROAD TRIP 03 – GERMANY, SPEED AND PERFORMANCE
Main photo © Dominic Fraser
Audi S8 Plus © Audi AG
Koenigsegg One:1 © Axion23
Porsche 918 Spyder (left) © Thom van der Noord | Photography
Porsche 918 Spyder (right) © Fabian Baege
Audi R8 V10 Plus © Audi AG
Bugatti Veyron 16.4 Grand Sport Vitesse © Dominic Fraser

ROAD TRIP 04 – ALPINE ADVENTURE
Main photo © Ultimate Drives
Porsche Cayman GT4 © Sebastian T Photography
McLaren 570S © McLaren Automotive Ltd.
Ferrari 488 GTB © Westbroek Car Spotting
Mercedes AMG GT S © Daimler AG
Lamborghini Huracán LP610-4 © Lorenz Richard

ROAD TRIP 05 – DESIGNS ON ITALY
Main photo © George F Williams
Ferrari LaFerrari © Axion23
Pagani Zonda S © Sebastian T Photography
Lamborghini Miura SV © George F Williams
SCG 003 S © Daniel Stocker
Alfa Romeo 8C Competizione © Fiat Chrysler Automobiles N.V.
Ferrari F40 © George F Williams

ROAD TRIP 06 – MONACO, BABY!
Main photo © Kevin Stec
Rolls-Royce Dawn © Rolls-Royce Motor Cars
Ferrari 250 GTO © Kevin Stec
Renault Twizy © Julien Hubert Photographie
Ferrari 458 Speziale © Sebastian T Photography
Mercedes-Benz 300 SL Gullwing © Raphaël Belly Photography

ROAD TRIP 07 – DUBAI DREAM
Main photo © Sebastian T Photography
Koenigsegg Regera © JamesHolm.se
Lamborghini Veneno © Sebastian T Photography
Mercedes-Benz G 63 AMG © Daimler AG
Pagani Huayra © Arun M Nair Photography
Mercedes-Benz SLR McLaren Stirling Moss © Alexandre Prevot Photographie
Maserati MC12 © Sebastian T Photography

ROAD TRIP 08 – DESERT OUTRUN
Main photo © George F Williams
Mercedes-Benz G 63 AMG 6x6 © Daimler AG
W Motors Lykan Hypersport © W Motors shot by JamesHolm.se
Lamborghini Aventador LP700-4 © Patrick3331
Aston Martin One-77 © Alexandre Prevot Photographie
Porsche Carrera GT © Jens Lucking Photography

ROAD TRIP 09 – INTO THE EAST
Main photo © Toyota Motor Corporation
Lexus LFA © Toyota Motor Corporation
Nissan GT-R Nismo © Nissan Motor Company Ltd
Honda NSX © Honda Motor Co Ltd
Lamborghini Murciélago © Damian Morys Photography
Nissan Skyline R34 GT-R © Sng Wie Jie (E3lipse Photography)

ROAD TRIP 10 – WEST COAST AMERICA
Main Photo © Tesla Motors inc.
Tesla Model S P90D © Tesla Motors inc.
Ford GT © Ford Motor Company
SSC Ultimate Aero © Nate Hawbaker
Mustang Eleanor © BliniKord-GmbH
Hennessey Venom GT © HPE DESIGN LLC

ROAD TRIP 11 – EAST COAST AMERICA
Main photo © Nick Dimbleby
Range Rover Autobiography © Jaguar Land Rover Limited
Ferrari Testarossa © George F Williams
Rolls-Royce Wraith © Rolls-Royce Motor Cars
Bentley Continental GT V8 S © Bentley Motors Limited shot
by James Lipman
Cadillac CTS-V © General Motors Company

ROAD TRIP 12 – MAKING TRACKS IN PORTUGAL
Main photo © General Motors Company
McLaren P1 © McLaren Automotive Limited
Porsche 911 GT3 RS © Dr. Ing. h.c. F. Porsche AG
Chevrolet Corvette Z06 © General Motors Company
McLaren 675LT © McLaren Automotive Limited
Ferrari F12tdf © George F Williams
BAC Mono © Will Aron's Photography

ROAD TRIP 13 – FRANCE AND FURIOUS
Main photo © Raphaël Belly Photography
Pagani Zonda R © Nicolas Leung-Tack
Ferrari FXX K © Nicolas Speck Photographie
Aston Martin Vulcan © Max Earey
McLaren P1 GTR © McLaren Automotive Ltd.
Lamborghini Sesto Elemento © Automobili Lamborghini S.p.A.

ROAD TRIP 14 – BEST OF BRITISH
Main photo © Morgan Motor Company shot by G F Williams
& Bruce Holder
Lotus Evora 400 © GROUP LOTUS PLC
Caterham Seven 620S © Caterham Cars
Morgan Aero 8 © Morgan Motor Company shot by G F Williams
& Bruce Holder
Zenos E10 S © Zenos Cars Limited
Ariel Atom 500 © Ariel Motor Company Ltd
Morgan 3 Wheeler © Morgan Motor Company shot by
G F Williams & Bruce Holder